Notes / E

Krishna Bista, *Executive Editor*
Morgan State University, USA

Chris R. Glass, *Editor-In-Chief*
Old Dominion University, USA

Special Issue on

**Reflection and Reflective Thinking on
International Student**

Special Issue Co-Editors:

Mary Ryan
Macquarie University, Australia
Georgina Barton
University of Southern Queensland, Australia

Vol. **10** Issue **S2** November 2020

JOURNAL OF INTERNATIONAL STUDENTS

A Quarterly Publication on International Education

Access this journal online at: http://ojed.org/jis

Copyright © 2020 by *Journal of International Students*

All rights reserved. This journal is a STAR Scholars Network publication.

Print ISSN 2162-3104
Online ISSN 2166-3750

Disclaimer
Facts and opinions published in *Journal of International Students* (JIS) express solely the opinions of the respective authors. Authors are responsible for their citing of sources and the accuracy of their references and bibliographies. The editors cannot be held responsible for any lacks or possible violations of third parties' rights.

Special Issue on
Reflection and Reflective Thinking (2020)
Special Issue Co-Editors:
Georgina Barton, University of Southern Queensland, Australia
Mary Ryan, Macquarie University, Australia

Special Issue | *Bahasa Indonesia* on
International Students and COVID-19 (2020)
Special Issue Co-Editors:
Handoyo Puji Widodo, King Abdulaziz University, Saudi Arabia
Sandi Ferdiansyah, Institut Agama Islam Negeri, Indonesia and
Lara Fridani, Universitas Negeri Jakarta, Indonesia

Special Issue | *Chinese* on
International Students in China (2020)
Special Issue Co-Editors: *Mei Tian and Genshu Lu*
Xi'an Jiaotong University, China

Special Issue on
**Fostering Successful Integration and Engagement Between
Domestic and International Students** (2018)
Special Issue Co-Editors: *CindyAnn Rose-Redwood and Reuben Rose-
Redwood, University of Victoria, Canada*

Special Issue on
**The Role of Student Affairs in International Student Transition and
Success** (2017)
Special Issue Co-Editors:
Christina W Yao, University of Nebraska-Lincoln, US
Chrystal A. George Mwangi, University of Massachusetts Amherst, US

Special Issue on
International Student Success (2016)
Special Issue Editor: *Rahul Choudaha, DrEducation, United States*

Emerson is a campus without borders.

We believe producing inspired work requires a global perspective, which is why the Emerson experience isn't limited to one city or even one country. As a global hub of arts and communication in higher education, we strive to provide our students, faculty, and staff with opportunities to connect and collaborate across countries and cultures. From our Global Pathways Programs to our castle in the Netherlands and beyond, we offer more than opportunities for students to study abroad—we provide access to enriching cultural experiences that will guide you on the path to becoming a global citizen.

Emerson
COLLEGE

Our newest global degree programs:

- **Global BA in Business of Creative Enterprises: Australia**
  Our accelerated Global BA in Business of Creative Enterprises (BCE) is powered by a rich management-focused curriculum; immerses students in the life of companies and organizations across two continents through intensive internship programs; and spans venues in **Sydney**, **Boston**, and **Los Angeles**.

- **Global BFA in Film Art**
  Our intercontinental joint Global BFA in Film Art spans venues in **Paris**, **the Netherlands**, and **Boston**. In this one-of-a-kind degree program, students will not only study visual and media arts in the City of Light itself, but will also receive a foundation in the liberal arts and French language.

Learn more at **emerson.edu/global**.

Routledge Studies in Global Student Mobility Series

This Routledge Series offers a scholarly forum for original and innovative research to understand the issues and challenges as well as share the best practices related to international student mobility in K-12 and beyond, education abroad, and exchange programs globally that creates a professional network of researchers and practitioners.

https://www.routledge.com/posts/15842

Series Editors
Dr. Chris R. Glass & Dr. Krishna Bista,
For questions and submission, email at crglass@odu.edu

Forthcoming Titles

Inequalities in Study Abroad and Student Mobility: Challenges and Practices

Student Mobilities and the Global South

International Student Employability from the Global South

Social Mobility in Higher Education

International Students in Community Colleges

International Student Support and Engagement

International Faculty in Institutions of Higher Education

International Students in the Middle East: Comparative Critical Perspectives

ISSN: 2162-3104 Print/ ISSN: 2166-3750 Online
2020 Volume 10, Number S2
© *Journal of International Students*
http://ojed.org/jis

Editorial Team

Founder/Executive Editor
Krishna Bista, Morgan State University, USA

Editor-in-Chief
Chris R. Glass, Old Dominion University, USA

Senior Copy Editor
Joy Bancroft, Emporia State University, USA

Managing Editor
Laura Soulsby, Old Dominion University, USA

Production Editor
Natalie Cruz, Old Dominion University, USA

Book Review Editor
Lisa Unangst, Boston College, USA

EDITORIAL ADVISORY BOARD (2019-2022)

- Dr. Darla Deardorff, Research Fellow, *Duke University, USA*
- Dr. Margaret Kettle, Associate Professor, *Queensland U. of Technology, Australia*
- Dr. David Di Maria, Associate VP for International Education, *UMBC, USA*
- Dr. Aneta Hayes, Director of Programs (UG and MA), *Keele University, UK*
- Dr. Rahul Choudaha, Principal Researcher, *DrEducation, USA*
- Dr. Catherine Gomes, Associate Professor, *RMIT University, Australia*
- Dr. Rajika Bhandari, *Senior Advisor, Institute of International Education, USA*
- Dr. Helen Forbes-Mewett, Deputy Director, MMIC *Monash University, Australia*
- Dr. Nigel Harwood, Reader in Applied Linguistics, *University of Sheffield, UK*
- Dr. Anthony Ogden, Associate VP for Global Engagement, *U. of Wyoming, USA*
- Dr. Bojana Petric, Head of Dept. of ALC, Birkbeck *University of London, UK*
- Dr. Megan M. Siczek, Director of EAP, *The George Washington University, USA*
- Dr. Lily Lei Ye, Associate Professor, *Beijing Institute of Fashion Tech, China*
- Dr. Ly Tran, Associate Professor, *Deakin University, Australia*
- Dr. Lydia Andrade, Professor, *University of the Incarnate Word, USA*
- Dr. Stuart Tannock, Senior Lecturer, *University College London, UK*

- Dr. Lien Pham, *Lecturer, University of Technology Sydney, Australia*
- Dr. Janet Ilieva, Founder/Director, *Education Insight*, UK
- Dr. Yingyi Ma, Associate Professor, *Syracuse University, USA*
- Dr. Nicolai Netz, *German Center for Higher Education Research and Science Studies (DZHW), Germany*

Associate Editors (2019-2021)

- Dr. Nelson Brunsting, *Wake Forest University, USA*
- Dr. Kun Dai, *Peking Univeristy, China*
- Dr. Helen Forbes-Mewett, *Monash University, Australia*
- Dr. Hugo Garcia, *Texas Tech University, USA*
- Dr. Anesa Hosein, *University of Surrey, UK*
- Dr. Mingsheng Li, *Massey University, Wellington, New Zealand*
- Dr. Stephanie Kim, *Georgetown University, US*
- Dr. Yingyi Ma, Associate Professor, *Syracuse University, USA*
- Dr. Charles Mathies, *University of Jyväskylä, Finland*
- Dr. Mohammad Nurunnabi, *Prince Sultan University, Saudi Arabia*
- Dr. CindyAnn Rose-Redwood, *University of Victoria, Canada*
- Dr. Reuben Rose-Redwood, *University of Victoria, Canada*
- Dr. Christina Yao, *University of South Carolina, US*
- Dr. Yi-Leaf Zhang, *The University of Texas at Arlington, US*
- Dr. Helene Syed Zwick, *ESLSCA University, Egypt*

Assistant Editors (2019-2021)

- Dr. Sam Adeyemo, *University of Pretoria, South Africa*
- Dr. Jasper Kun-Ting Hsieh, *The University of New South Wales, Australia*
- Dr. Kayla Johnson, *University of Cincinnati, US*
- Dr. Katie Koo, *Texas A&M University – Commerce, US*
- Dr. Masha Krsmanovic, *University of Central Florida, US*
- Dr. Shu-Wen Lan, *National Pingtung U. of Science and Technology, Taiwan*
- Dr. Jiangnan Li, *Durham University, United Kingdom*
- Dr. Xi Lin, *East Carolina University, US*
- Dr. Fatma Mizikaci, *Ankara University, Turkey*
- Dr. Hiep Hung Pham, *Phu Xuan University, Viet Nam*
- Dr. Wonsun Ryu, *The University of Texas at Austin, US*
- Dr. ZW Taylor, *The University of Texas at Austin, US*
- Dr. Tiffany Viggiano, *University of Alaska, US*
- Dr. Melissa Whatley, *North Carolina State University, US*

JOURNAL OF
INTERNATIONAL
STUDENTS
2020 VOL. 10, NO. S3
Access this journal online at ojed.org/jis

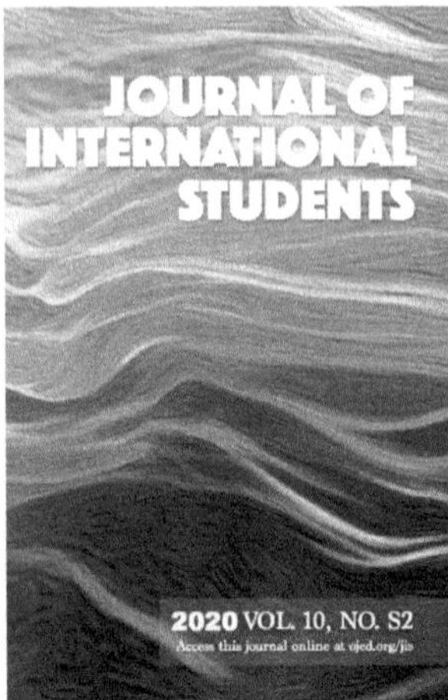
JOURNAL OF
INTERNATIONAL
STUDENTS
2020 VOL. 10, NO. S2
Access this journal online at ojed.org/jis

JOURNAL OF
INTERNATIONAL
STUDENTS
国际学生杂志 "来华留学生" 专刊
SPECIAL ISSUE ON INTERNATIONAL STUDENTS IN CHINA
2020 VOL. 10, NO. S1
Access this journal online at ojed.org/jis

JOURNAL OF
INTERNATIONAL
STUDENTS
2020 VOL. 10, NO. 4
Access this journal online at ojed.org/jis

JOURNAL OF
INTERNATIONAL
STUDENTS
2020 VOL. 10, NO. 3
Access this journal online at ojed.org/jis

JOURNAL OF
INTERNATIONAL
STUDENTS
2020 VOL. 10, NO. 2
Access this journal online at ojed.org/jis

JOURNAL OF
INTERNATIONAL
STUDENTS
2020 VOL. 10, NO. 1
Access this journal online at ojed.org/jis

JOURNAL OF
INTERNATIONAL
STUDENTS
2019 VOL. 9, NO. 4
Access this journal online at ojed.org/jis

JOURNAL OF
INTERNATIONAL
STUDENTS
2019 VOL. 9, NO. 3
Access this journal online at ojed.org/jis

Reviews

"This book is a valuable addition to our understanding of the relationship between inequalities and international education – both at home and abroad. Besides offering insights from cases around the Western world, all chapters also offer useful implications for daily practice."
Christof Van Mol, Assistant Professor, Tilburg University, Netherlands

"Inequalities in Study Abroad and Student Mobility presents a remarkable set of voices that, taken together, provide a deep, critical, and valuable analysis of some of the most pressing issues for international higher education."
Gerardo L. Blanco, Associate Professor, Boston College, USA

"The COVID-19 crisis made the risk of growing inequalities in higher education even more visible. *Inequalities in Study Abroad and Student Mobility* is a must-read book addressing the topic of inequalities in internationalization and study abroad in a holistic manner.
Giorgio Marinoni, Manager, International Association of Universities, France

"An impressive and important collection. The editors have assembled twelve strong contributions that not only lay out the challenges inherent in study abroad access in an unbalanced and vulnerable world, but offer well-reasoned prescriptions for greater equity, effectiveness, and sustainable positive impact.
James E. Callaghan, Assistant Vice-President, Georgia College & State University, USA

OPEN JOURNALS IN EDUCATION

High-quality, peer-reviewed academic journals based at leading universities worldwide.

Open Journals in Education (OJED) publishes high quality peer reviewed, open access journals based at research universities. OJED uses the Open Journal System (OJS) platform, where readers can browse by subject, drill down to journal level to find the aims, scope, and editorial board for each individual title, as well as search back issues. OJED journals are required to be indexed in major academic databases to ensure quality and maximize article discoverability and citation. Journals follow best practices on publication ethics outlined in the COPE Code of Conduct. Explore our OJED Journals at www.ojed.org

***

A. Noam Chomsky Global Connections Awards celebrate the power of human connections. The awards recognize distinguished service to the global mission of the STAR Scholars Network. Several individuals with a deep impact on advancing global, social mobility are recognized every year.

For more information, visit https://starscholars.org/global-connections-award/

Indexing

ISSN: 2162-3104 Print/ ISSN: 2166-3750 Online
Journal of International Students
http://ojed.org/jis

All articles published in the *Journal of International Students* are indexed and listed in major databases and sources:

SUBJECT: EDUCATION – HIGHER   DEWEY # 378

CEDROM SNI
- Eureka.cc, 01/01/2017-
- Europresse.com, 01/01/2017-

Directory of Open Access Journals
- Directory of Open Access Journals, 2011-

EBSCOhost
- Education Source, 03/01/2012-

Gale
- Academic OneFile, 09/01/2011-
- Contemporary Women's Issues, 09/01/2011-
- Educator's Reference Complete, 09/01/2011-
- Expanded Academic ASAP, 09/01/2011-
- InfoTrac Custom, 09/01/2011-

Multiple Vendors
- Freely Accessible Social Science Journals, 2011-

ProQuest
- Education Collection, 10/01/2011-
- Education Database, 10/01/2011-
- Education Database (Alumni Edition), 10/01/2011-
- ProQuest Central, 10/01/2011-
- ProQuest Central - UK Customers, 10/01/2011-
- ProQuest Central (Alumni Edition), 10/01/2011-
- ProQuest Central (Corporate), 10/01/2011-
- ProQuest Central (US Academic Subscription), 10/01/2011-
- ProQuest Central China, 10/01/2011-
- ProQuest Central Essentials, 10/01/2011-
- ProQuest Central Korea, 10/01/2011-
- ProQuest Central Student, 10/01/2011-
- ProQuest Research Library, 10/01/2011-
- ProQuest Research Library (Corporate), 10/01/2011-
- ProQuest Social Sciences Premium Collection, 10/01/2011-
- ProQuest Social Sciences Premium Collection - UK Customers, 10/01/2011-
- Research Library (Alumni Edition), 10/01/2011-
- Research Library China, 10/01/2011-
- Research Library Prep, 10/01/2011-
- Social Science Premium Collection, 10/01/2011-

Clarivate Analytics
- Web of Science
- Emering Sciences Citation Index
- Higher Education Abstracts

Source: Ulrichsweb Global Serials Directory

You may access the print and/or digital copies of the *Journal of International Students* from 586 libraries worldwide (as of Nov 8, 2020).

The Journal of International Students (Print ISSN 2162-3104 & Online ISSN 2166-3750) is a member of the STAR Scholars Network Open Journals in Education (OJED), a OJS 3 platform for *high-quality, peer-reviewed* academic journals in education.

JIS is a Gold Open Access journal and indexed in major academic databases to maximize article discoverability and citation. JIS follows best practices on publication ethics outlined in the COPE Code of Conduct. Editors work to ensure timely decisions after initial submission, as well as prompt publication online if a manuscript is accepted for publication.

Upon publication articles are immediately and freely available to the public. The final version of articles can immediately be posted to an institutional repository or to the author's own website as long as the article includes a link back to the original article posted on OJED.

None of the OJED journals charge fees to individual authors thanks to the generous support of our institutional sponsors.

For further information

Editorial Office
Journal of International Students
URL: http://ojed.org/jis
E-mail: contact@jistudents.org

ISSN: 2162-3104 Print/ ISSN: 2166-3750 Online
2020 Volume 10, Number S2
© *Journal of International Students*
http://ojed.org/jis

TABLE OF CONTENTS

Editorial
Special Edition | Reflection and Reflective Thinking

© *Journal of International Students*
Volume 10, Issue S2 (202X), pp. i-v
ISSN: 2162-3104 (Print), 2166-3750 (Online)
ojed.org/jis

International Students, Reflection, and Employability

Mary Ryan
Macquarie University, Australia

Georgina Barton
University of Southern Queensland, Australia

ABSTRACT

International students make an incredibly important contribution to universities worldwide. It is therefore critical that higher education contexts support international students' success in their studies. The International Student Barometer indicates international students' interest in work experience, career advice and employment post-study. A necessary skill for all graduates is the ability to be able to reflect on and in professional practice, yet there is limited research that explores reflection, the teaching of reflective thinking, and reflexivity for international students. Our research has shown that international students may approach the process of reflection differently due to their cultural differences so it is important that universities acknowledge and consider further ways in which to teach and assess reflection for international students. This special issue shares 7 papers related to international students and reflection by drawing on Rodgers' four functions of reflection. We hope that the special issue is of value to the journal's readership, particularly in regard to assisting both academic and support staff in universities with their work on reflection with international students.

Keywords: international students, reflection, reflexivity, employability

In this special issue we explore the importance of reflection and reflective thinking for international students in a range of contexts. For many educational programs in universities, reflection and reflective thinking are critical skills required to meet graduate attributes and professional standards, ensuring employability (Treleaven & Voola, 2008). Even though there is a significant amount of research that has explored the importance of reflection in the higher education context (Moon, 2001; Smith, 2011), including in specific discipline areas (Barton & Ryan, 2013; Mann et al., 2009), there is limited scholarly work that addresses how international students reflect or what approaches to teaching and assessing reflection might best support international students for post-study employment.

The editors of this special issue have conducted prior research on reflection and international students noting that reflection is a "common expectation for learners in higher education, both informally in the hope that learners will reflect and act upon feedback provided and also in formal assessment tasks and work integrated learning experiences" (Barton & Ryan, 2017, p. 93). However, higher education contexts and workplaces may assume and implement set approaches to reflection for all students which might not align with international students' understanding and knowledge about reflective practice. In some of our work on reflection in higher education we explored multimodal methods, arguing that different disciplines may also view reflection in different ways (Barton & Ryan, 2013). It is critical that higher educators consider culturally-appropriate ways to reflect for international students as this acknowledges and embraces diverse ways of thinking.

It is still important to define reflection when comprehending different ways to think and act reflectively. Hatton and Smith's (1995) early work in teacher education presented a number of definitions of reflection, arguing some difficulty in pinning down an absolute definition. They drew on foundational work by Dewey (1993) and offered different perspectives and purposes of reflection from the literature. These included reflection as critical thought versus practice (Gore & Zeichner, 1991; Schön, 1983, 1987), problem solving (Adler, 1991; Calderhead, 1989) and strategies to teach reflection. They conclude by sharing different purposes of reflection including reflecting *in* and *on* action (Schön, 1983) and reflection as a technical rationality (Van Manen, 1977) in which certain decision making processes are engaged. They argue that reflective practice can be shared by students descriptively, dialogically and/or critically.

For the purpose of this special issue Rodgers (2002) four functions of reflection will be explored in each paper. These functions include reflection as: a meaning-making process, a rigorous way of thinking, being important in and for community and, a set of attitudes. Authors have also considered other models where appropriate. The Special Issue explores how the four functions might look different in these diverse contexts. Basing each chapter on a specific framework such as Rodgers (2002), allows an in-depth examination of diverse reflective practices. We are also interested in knowing not only the different ways teachers of international students teach reflection and how international students reflect, but also how these attributes contribute to international students' preparedness for work experience as well as the implications for employability post-graduation.

Contributors come from a range of countries and contexts and have been involved in comprehensive work with international students for some time. They are committed to embedding the practice of reflection when working with international students throughout their studies. As stated previously, a significant amount of scholarly work focuses on how to improve learning teaching and learning in higher education related to reflection, however, there is limited research exploring reflection and reflective thinking when working with international students. We believe that it is critical to consider reflective practices and its affordances for international students, given their importance in many universities globally.

The Special Issue takes a strengths-based rather than a deficit view of this topic as international students bring unique perspectives and capacities for learning and employment in and beyond higher education contexts. Barton and Ryan lead off the issue with a conceptualization of what reflective thinking and reflexive practice look and feel like for international students. They illustrate the importance of contextually relevant strategies to enable success and employability for international students with diverse and complex needs and goals. In the second paper, Snepvangers and O'Rourke explore the collaborative dynamics of international students, staff and industry partners using a community building framework for work integrated learning (WIL) to simulate the 'gig economy'. They focus on the development of transferable skills of creative and critical thinking through intercultural learning and show how to plan an academic creative practice WIL program for mentors. Uusimaki and Garvis use reflections to understand how international students studying in Sweden experience course structures, learning and teaching practices and relationship development with their lecturers. Despite a growth in international students in Sweden, there is a dearth of research in this area. They found that expectations differ across countries and it is important to provide induction sessions that include approaches to learning and teaching, and building relationships with academic staff.

Multi-socialization is a reality that many international students face (Barton et al., 2017). Socializing into a new country, a new culture, a new university setting, and sometimes, a new WIL setting, means that reflection is essential to manage the demands of multiple expectations. The fourth paper, by Hartwig, Stokhof and Fransen, investigates multi-socialization for teacher education students in The Netherlands. They found that reflection enabled students in their development as global citizens and global teachers. Finn, Phillipson and Goff similarly report on international teacher education students. In contrast, however, their participants engaged in a simulated practicum classroom experience in Australia. They investigated how international students drew on their cultural identities to reflect on their teaching practice. International students in this study negotiated the intersections of culture and pedagogy in diverse school classrooms, within the 'safe space' of a virtual reality simulation. Such an experience does, however, require an additional level of socialization into a virtual space.

The final two papers in this special issue focus on employability for international students. In the sixth paper, Fakunle and Pirrie explore international students' perceptions of developing their employability while studying in the UK. The draw discursive connections between internationalization and employability, two concepts that tend to be disconnected in policy and discourse. They recommend a more systemic approach to embedding employment development opportunities in courses. The final paper, by Watson and Barton, seems most timely in the current COVID-19 pandemic. It focuses on international students' wellbeing and employability using arts-based methods to help them think positively about their studies and future working lives. They found that arts-based methods of reflection enabled a 'community of respect' and prompted culturally appropriate sharing of challenges and what mattered most to these international students in the context of a global crisis.

Rodgers' four functions of reflection have proven to be a generative and illuminating framework to investigate the experiences of international students and academics around the world. This special issue demonstrates creative and critical approaches to reflection in different multi-socialization experiences. A common theme across these papers is the importance of explicitly embedding culturally-appropriate reflection into the learning of international students so they have the tools to negotiate the complex demands of international study in sustainable and fulfilling ways.

REFERENCES

Adler, S. (1991). The reflective practitioner and the curriculum of teacher education. *Journal of Education for Teaching, 17*(2), 139-150.

Barton, G. & Hartwig, K. (2017). *Professional learning in the work place for international students: Exploring theory and practice.* Cham, Switzerland: Springer.

Barton, G. M., & Ryan, M. (2013). Multimodal approaches to reflective teaching and assessment in higher education: a cross disciplinary approach in Creative Industries. *Higher Education Research and Development, 33*(3), 409-424.

Barton, G. M., Hartwig, K., Bennett, D., Cain, M., Campbell, M., Ferns, S., Jones, L., Joseph, D., Kavanagh, M., Kelly, A., Larkin, I., O'Connor, E., Podorova, A., Tangen, D., & Westerveld, M. (2017). Work placement for international students: A model of effective practice. In G. M. Barton & K. Hartwig (Eds.), *Professional Learning in the Work Place for International Students: Exploring Theory and Practice,* (pp. 13-34). Springer Publishers.

Barton, G. M., & Ryan, M.E. (2017). Reflection and reflective practice for international students and their supervisors in context. In G. M. Barton & K. Hartwig (Eds.), *Professional Learning in the Work Place for International Students: Exploring Theory and Practice,* (pp. 93-110). Springer Publishers.

Calderhead, J. (1989). Reflective teaching and teacher education. *Teaching and Teacher Education, 5*(1), 43-51.

Dewey, J. (1933). *How we think: A restatement of the relation of reflective thinking to the educative process, vol. 8.* Boston: D. C Heath

Gore, J. M., & Zeichner, K. M. (1991). Action research and reflective teaching in preservice teacher education: A case study from the United States. *Teaching and Teacher Education, 7*(2), 119-136.

Hatton, N., & Smith, D. (1995). Reflection in teacher education: Towards definition and implementation. *Teaching and Teacher Education, 11*(1), 33-49.

Mann, K., Gordon, J., & MacLeod, A. (2009). Reflection and reflective practice in health professions education: a systematic review. *Advances in Health Sciences Education, 14*(4), 595-621.

Moon, J. (2001). PDP working paper 4: Reflection in higher education learning. *Higher Education Academy*, 1-25.

Rodgers, C. (2002). Defining reflection: Another look at John Dewey and reflective thinking. *Teachers College Record, 104*(4), 842-866.

Schön, D. A. (1983). *The reflective practitioner: How professionals think in action.* New York: Basic Books, Inc.

Schön, D. A. (1987). *Educating the reflective practitioner.* San Francisco: Jossey-Bass.

Smith, E. (2011). Teaching critical reflection. *Teaching in Higher Education, 16*(2), 211-223.

Treleaven, L., & Voola, R. (2008). Integrating the development of graduate attributes through constructive alignment. *Journal of Marketing Education, 30*(2), 160-173.

Van Manen, M. (1977). Linking ways of knowing with ways of being practical. *Curriculum Inquiry, 6*(3), 205-228.

MARY RYAN, PhD, is Professor and Dean of Education at Macquarie University, Sydney, Australia. Her research is in the areas of teachers' work in, and preparation for, diverse classrooms, reflexive learning and practice, writing pedagogy and assessment and reflective writing. She led a highly successful Australian Learning and Teaching Council grant (2010/11) on reflective learning across disciplines in higher education. Her current Australian Research Council Discovery projects are in the areas of classroom writing and preparing reflexive teachers for diverse classrooms. She is a Principal Fellow of the Higher Education Academy in the UK. Email: mary.ryan@mq.edu.au

GEORGINA BARTON, PhD, is a Professor and Associate Head – Research in the School of Education at the University of Southern Queensland, Brisbane, Australia. Before being an academic, Georgina taught in schools for over 20 years including teaching English in South India with Australian Volunteers International. Georgina also has extensive experience in teaching the arts in schools and universities and often utilizes the arts to support students' literacy learning outcomes. She has over 130 publications including as the lead editor of a book titled *Professional Learning for International Students: Exploring Theory and Practice.* She is a Principal Fellow of the Higher Education Academy in the UK. Email: georgina.barton@usq.edu.au

Peer-Reviewed Article
Special Edition | Reflection and Reflective Thinking

© *Journal of International Students*
Volume 10, Issue S2 (2020), pp. 1-16
ISSN: 2162-3104 (Print), 2166-3750 (Online)
ojed.org/jis

What Does Reflection Look and Feel Like for International Students? An Exploration of Reflective Thinking, Reflexivity and Employability

Georgina Barton
University of Southern Queensland, Australia

Mary Ryan
Macquarie University, Australia

ABSTRACT

Reflection, reflective thinking and reflexivity have received significant attention in the scholarly literature on higher education yet there is limited research that explores these concepts in relation to international students. This paper consequently explores what reflection and reflective thinking might look and feel like for international students. We theorize the importance of supporting international students in becoming reflexive practitioners in their chosen area of study; particularly in respect to graduate attributes including reflection and employability. The paper attends to this theorization by sharing Rodgers' (2002) four functions of reflection, a reflective thinking model – the 4Rs – as well as Archer's (2000, 2012) notion of reflexivity. We explore how higher educators might consider these frameworks comprehensively when working with international students particularly in the area of workplace experience.

Keywords: reflection, reflective thinking, reflexivity, international students, employability

---

Reflection and reflective thinking are consistently acknowledged as being essential for personal and professional growth (Korthagen & Vasalos, 2005; Moon, 2013). In the higher education context, this is specifically important for students throughout their professional studies as well as upon graduation for employability (de Schepper

1

& Sotiriadou, 2018). While there is significant scholarly literature exploring reflection in higher education there is limited research on how reflection might look and feel for international students (Barton & Ryan, 2017). Given international students are likely to have diverse cultural and social perspectives on learning, reflection may also be understood and enacted differently. Starr-Glass (2017) cautions against generic labelling of international students as a homogenous approach may ignore diverse perspectives and needs. Reflective practices for learning can enable a deep intercultural engagement whereby international students can consider their own backgrounds, experiences, perspectives and needs in relation to the contextual emergences of the institution and country that they have joined (Barton & Ryan, 2017).

In this paper we define the notions of reflection, reflective thinking and reflexivity within diverse sociocultural contexts. We theorize these concepts by asking what does reflection look and feel like for international students? And how can this information be considered by higher educators when working with international students, particularly in the areas of work placement and employability? We then share data from interviews with international students who have undertaken work placements in a range of contexts. Findings show that international students often face adverse circumstances that are specific to their cohort and therefore approaches to learning and teaching, including reflection, must be culturally-appropriate and -responsive. Further, we share how international students tend to reflect on practice in varied ways including seeking assistance from other international students, their friends and families back home, as well as by implementing different approaches to their studies to ensure success in their desired goal of employment (Garrett, 2014). We argue that if higher educators are made aware of these distinct differences and learning needs, then the challenges international students face may be overcome through effective reflective practice. A number of recommended strategies are shared to support higher educators in this work.

REFLECTION AND DIVERSITY

Reflection at a broad level, has been acknowledged as being difficult to define perhaps because it can have multiple purposes. Reflection for learning has been variously explicated from different perspectives and disciplines (see Boud, 1999; Ryan, 2013), but at the broad level, the definition we suggest as the most generative for international students' learning in higher education includes two key elements 1) making sense of experience in relation to self, others and contextual conditions; and importantly, 2) reimagining and/or planning future experience for personal, professional and social benefit. This definition reflects the belief that in order for international students to transform their learning and employability potential, they must engage in reflection that accounts for a rigorous examination of their beliefs and practices in relation to community, culture and professional futures. Using Rodgers (2002) four functions of reflection we highlight how students from different countries might think about each process. We draw on relevant literature in doing so.

Reflection as a meaning-making process for international students

International students undergo a multi-socialization process (Barton, Hartwig, et al., 2017) as they are required to socialize into a new country – which brings a range of unique cultural norms - a new university context, which can be quite different to their previous experience in the higher education sector - and a new work place environment. Such complex conditions can impact greatly on students' capacities to reflect. Reflection may be expressed differently depending on people's cultural and linguistic backgrounds as prior experience impacts on the ways in which we understand and deliberate about how and why we do things. Additionally, many scholars and practitioners have emphasized the important role reflection, and in particular self-reflection, plays for international and cross-cultural work and understanding (Furman, Coyne & Negi, 2008; Taylor, Ryan & Pearce, 2015). For example, Komins and Nicholls (2003) found reflection within diverse contexts allows deeper empathy towards others through a process of understanding "cultural and social realities other than one's own" (as cited in Schuldberg et al., 2012, p. 22). Others have also found that reflection assists with breaking down prejudices and resistance to cross-cultural educational practices (Khalili, Orchard, Spence Laschinger, & Farah, 2013). Reflection and reflective practice therefore, can be utilized to support students in understanding themselves, others and contexts, however, as a process, it can be executed differently.

An intercultural approach can take into account these differences so that multiple approaches to reflection and subsequent reformation of practice can happen within learning and work placement contexts. McAllister, Whiteford, Hill, Thomas and Fitzgerald (2006) offer a critical incident approach to enable higher education students to focus on a "continuum of intercultural learning" (p. 377) that explores key concepts of culture shock, challenging stereotypes, personal coping strategies and negotiating intercultural communication. Interculturalization is particularly important in work place components of students' programs. Not only do university staff need to consider and embed intercultural perspectives through a reflective process (Taylor et al., 2015) but so too, do work place staff. Of course, international students also need to participate and socialize into the work place environment by reflecting on the ways in which they engage with their mentor or supervisor/s but also their own practice in the quest to becoming work ready and employable.

In order to make and connect meanings in their specific learning contexts, international students can be explicitly taught how to reflect. Ryan & Ryan (2015), building on Bain, Ballantyne, Mills and Lester's (2009) work, outline how the 4Rs of reflective learning: reporting/responding, relating, reasoning, reconstructing can be a useful scaffold in higher education. These levels increase in complexity and move from description of, and personal response to, an issue or situation; to the use of theory and experience to explain, interrogate, and ultimately transform learning and practice. They suggest that the content or level of reflection should be determined by the problems and dilemmas of the practitioner. Using this framework, international students can be taught to *notice* (Rodgers, 2002) and deliberate about aspects of their own and others' learning and practice. They should be encouraged to form an opinion or have an initial emotional response to an issue or incident that is relevant to their discipline, the professional field or the learning space (reporting/relating). Self-dialogue can compare and contrast reflective, retrospective and prospective considerations (Ryan, 2015). Identifying and recounting incidents seems easy enough to do, however, it is crucial that the reflection has a clear focus if one intends to improve practice. An important part of making meaning through reflection is drawing on personal experiences (after Dewey, 1933) in relation to similar issues or contexts (relating). Students make connections with their skills and knowledge thus far, along with their values and priorities, and how these relate to the values and priorities of other stakeholders and of society more broadly. They can then begin to determine whether they have the skills and knowledge to deal with the issue (reasoning), whether to consult others or access resources and how to plan a way forward (reconstructing).

Reflection as a rigorous way of thinking for international students

Reasoning is a key element of the process of reflection that reduces an intellectually rigorous analysis of the context, the issue, and possible impacting factors. Ways of working within the discipline and the profession will determine the types of evidence or analysis that should be undertaken, and students' choice of evidence should demonstrate their knowledge of the discipline and the specific subject matter (Kienhues, Feucht, Ryan, M., & Weinstock, 2017). Opportunities to explain and discuss are useful strategies for students to examine different possibilities and sometimes consider ethical implications. Volet (2004) argued the importance of fostering critical reflection skills for international students so they can engage in one of the fundamental outcomes of a university education – engaging in social debate and critical thinking. This, she explained, opens up discourse related to the diverse nature of knowledge and alternative perspectives, ultimately addressing the distinct student and staff cohorts in higher education contexts.

Attention to epistemic cognition is a way to ensure rigor in reflective thinking. Epistemic cognition involves a process of individuals determining what they know as opposed to what they believe or distrust (Greene & Yu, 2016; Lunn Brownlee, Ferguson & Ryan, 2017). Further, Chinn, Buckland and Samarapungavan, 2011 point to the importance of knowledge, its sources and justification, belief, evidence, truth, understanding, and explanation as part of the rigor of knowing and thinking. Lunn Brownlee, Ferguson and Ryan (2017) argue that explicit reflection on epistemic beliefs can enable students and teachers in higher education to more rigorously justify their knowledge, their understandings and how they might apply these in different contexts.

Rigorous reflective processes should not be left to chance. It is not always clear to students why they have been successful (or not) in learning tasks, or whether particular choices are effective (or not). An understanding of how students learn in different ways is paramount, and part of this understanding relates to helping students to understand themselves, their epistemic cognitions and how they learn. In this way, they can become self-analytical and independent learners as they move from higher education into the profession (Ryan, 2013; Sadler, 2010). Self-analysis in a learning situation requires a number of skills and capabilities. First, it is necessary to have an understanding of the requirements of the task and the requisite knowledge to complete it. Second, the implications of one's own investment in the task, including emotional investment is integral. Third, one must possess the ability to recognize or judge what constitutes reliable knowledge (Chinn et al., 2011) and quality in this particular context. Fourth, an understanding of the discourse of assessment feedback is an oft-forgotten yet crucial aspect of learning in formal educational settings (Ryan, 2015). These capabilities can be made visible (and can be targeted by teachers) through critical reflection as part of the learning cycle. Sadler (2010) argues that we need to provide students with substantial evaluative experience not as an extra but as a strategic part of the teaching design.

Reflection as being important in and for community

In unpacking reflection in community more thoroughly, Rodgers (2002) revisits John Dewey's notion that effective reflection for, and with, community purposes requires one to get outside of an experience and see it as another would see it. This aligns with Hunter, Pearson and Gutierrez's (2015) idea of interculturalization as a process where you think about others first, yourself second. For international students this process is critical – to ensure that they consider their own knowledge, experience and learning in relation to the learning community and its social and cultural functions. Community can be conceived of in different ways for international students: It includes the social and cultural community of the host country, the community values and practices of the specific university, and the ways of knowing in the disciplinary community in the student's area of study.

Freebody, Maton and Martin (2008) argue that the ways of working within disciplines will vary according to key topics, social and cultural functions, and the ways in which knowledge is generated and represented. These values and philosophies about how knowledge is generated (Kienhues et al., 2017), its purposes and cultural functions, also determine the kinds of 'texts' that are consumed and produced and the type of reflective activity that is valued. Moje (2008) argues that students should learn how to enact particular *identities* in different disciplines. She suggests that teachers need to provide opportunities for students to develop meta-discursive skills, whereby they not only engage in the different discourse communities of the different disciplines, but they also know how and why they are engaging and what those engagements mean for them and others in terms of social positioning and power relations. This is particularly pertinent for international students in professional contexts, which are steeped in particular disciplines and which prioritize particular types of knowledge, skills and relationships.

Reflection as a set of attitudes for international students

Lifelong learning is transformative, that is, it involves a weighing up of frames of reference and assumptions (including one's own) and being open to changing one's perspective or ideas (Mezirow 2006). Given that our frames of reference are continually and rapidly changing, there is no longer a blueprint from the past or from others that we can reliably draw upon to guide future actions (Archer, 2012). The changing relationship between social structures and culture, that is, they are both changing and being changed by each other, means that we are now in a time of unprecedented contextual incongruity where variety produces more variety (Archer 2012). Individuals are faced with multiple possible pathways, choices and outcomes. For example, students decide how much effort they will put into an assignment, based on how interested they are in the subject matter, how well they understand the task, how many other assignments they have, how much time they have available, how much the task is worth to their overall grade, what they know about the marker and so on. Students have choices within the structures of university policies and procedures, but of course these policies and procedures also shape choices around assessment. Students deliberate about their learning journey constantly but may not be conscious of how and why they make decisions and what cultural, professional or disciplinary knowledge they may be missing (Ryan, 2013). Making these deliberations more visible and self-conscious, can lead to more effective decision-making and the capacity for lifelong learning. Lifelong learning is not just a process; it is also an attitude to ongoing improvement. The key to successful strategies for lifelong learning is to provide well-scaffolded opportunities for reflective thought and reflexive learning. These opportunities optimally include identifying issues or concerns, weighing up their importance and the reliability of one's knowledge and skills to deal with them, reasoning about the implications of particular actions (using various forms of evidence), and deciding on the most appropriate course of action which is both satisfying and sustainable. If higher education teachers include explicit reflective dimensions in learning and assessment which foreground ongoing self-analysis, students are more likely to be able to diagnose issues and improve learning (Lunn Brownlee et al., 2017). Well-designed reflective opportunities should involve demonstration and application of disciplinary and professional knowledge, but with added expectations of adaptability and agility necessary for the professional context.

WHAT REFLECTION LOOKS AND FEELS LIKE FOR INTERNATIONAL STUDENTS IN RELATION TO WORK PLACEMENT

In this section of the paper we share data from a large-scale research project about international students and work placement (2014-2016)[1] and an extension study that focused on international students' volunteering experiences in various work places (2018-2019)[2]. The aforementioned study known as the *Work Placement for International Student Programs* (WISP) project aimed to investigate what international students experienced before, during and after workplace experiences in their studies. The project included international students in the fields of Business, Education, Engineering, and a range of health professions including Nursing, Occupational Therapy, Psychology and Speech Pathology. Across the three years of

---

[1] The WISP project was funded by the Office for Learning and Teaching (OLT) in Australia. This paper may not reflect the views of the OLT.
[2] The IVA project was funded by Trade Investment Queensland, International Education and Training. This paper may not reflect the views of TIQ (IET)

the project over 80 international students, 20 work place supervisors and 45 university staff responsible for work placement participated in interviews and close to 300 international students answered a survey. The second study, *International Volunteers Australia* (IVA), involved 12 international students undertaking a short volunteering experience in business and education with local industry partners. The aim of this study was to identify how these volunteering experiences assisted international students in becoming workplace ready for more formal professional experiences in their study programs.

For the purpose of this paper, we have used both deductive and inductive thematic analysis strategies when analyzing international student interview data. The analysis aimed to identify the role reflection played in their discussions about work placement and volunteering in different workplaces. The initial analysis involved identification of common themes revealed across all data. According to Braun and Clarke (2006) "a theme captures something important about the data in relation to the research question, and represents some level of patterned response or meaning within the data set" (p. 82). In relation to the deductive thematic analysis we identified what level of reflection the students used from a re-adapted version of the 4Rs model of reflection (Barton & Ryan, 2014) when discussing each theme. This allowed us to detail what aspects and types of reflection were important for international students in differing circumstances. Our analysis revealed the following areas of interest and concern at the forefront of international students' experience and thinking: financial situation, cultural and language differences, and areas or lack of support. We explore each of these in detail as well as comment on the levels of reflection undertaken by the students.

Financial aspects

Overwhelmingly, international students indicated the financial challenges when undertaking study in overseas locations. They would often *report* on the challenge of having to work either part-time while studying, even during work placement blocks. This meant that some students were attending work placement during the day for up to 9 weeks and working in the evenings to ensure they still had an income. Such a situation put enormous pressure on international students. They *reported* being extremely tired, especially if they had long travel times to their work place environment. Ishmael for example noted:

> *I have been so busy that I haven't been able to buy groceries so I am living on 2 minute noodles at the moment. I mean, I guess if I was home I would have friends and family supporting me but here I have to do everything myself...The travel time is really impacting as I have to leave home at 6am and don't get back until 8 or 9 at night.* (Ishmael, Psychology student)

John also noted the difficulty of having to plan for their professional experience while at the same time having to support themselves during the block period, often up to 6 full-time weeks, in schools.

> *It's just harder for financial reasons. It costs a lot of money when you're an international student...and during the prac I needed to earn some money. So it's really hard because you have to plan the lessons for the day after, but you also have to work* (John, Education student).

In addition to the financial hardships faced, international students consistently *reasoned* that it was important to complete their work placement as they *reported* on their strong desire to find work in Australia post-study. They *reasoned* about their choice to study overseas with the goal of gaining employment but also *related* this goal to the difficulties associated with money, visa restrictions, and racism.

> *I wanted to study in Australia as I want to work here after finishing. I have tried to get some employment but it is really difficult. I think people don't like having international students working with them. I don't know – maybe it is because of our accents or the fact that we may not be able to stay here after study as it is difficult to get working visas.* (Sunil, Business student)

Considering the financial circumstances of international students, three levels of reflection were undertaken – reporting, relating and reasoning. There was no evidence of the students reconstructing this situation, which is understandable given they were mostly supporting themselves financially through the study. While domestic students may have a similar outcome it is important to recognize that international students do not have access to financial support through agencies such as the Australian government's Centre Link.

Cultural and language differences

Many of the international students mentioned issues pertaining to cultural and/or language differences. It is important to note that not all of the international students interviewed were English as Second Language (ESL) learners. In fact, some students were from English speaking countries and others were multi-lingual with English being an additional language (EAL). A predominant experience of the international students was related to the ways in which work was carried out in professional contexts. The students commented how this was often different to what they had either experienced back home or what they expected it to be like.

> *I was working in healthcare in [my own country] and we had very different ways of working with patients. I feel like my prior knowledge is not taken into account at all. I know a number of natural healing procedures for example, that just would never be used in Australian hospitals* (Nim, Nursing student)

> *We would never allow some of the behavior I have seen in classrooms here on my prac. I feel our teachers are much more stricter. I also did not know*

much about group work but I have learnt much more about this here in Australia. (Ying, Education student)

Nim was able to *relate* her experience to her prior knowledge back in her home country. She was also able to *reason* that her knowledge was not valued or drawn upon in her clinical placement due to different approaches in nursing education and health care in Australia. Ying also was able to relate her experience in the classroom to her own experience as a school student. She was able to *reason* that despite the behavioral issues faced in the classroom she also learnt about different pedagogical approaches to teaching.

In regard to language differences some of the students shared that they knew that people sometimes did not understand them due to their strong accents. Some were even trying to disguise these accents when in working conditions.

> *I was only Asian in the staff room so maybe you can imagine that in all female and I was only Asian. So I feel like I was excluded from the conversation but I would still feel welcomed if they asked for my opinion. Yeah, that was the thing, being an Asian and being a non-native English speaker so that was hard, just to fit in.* (Mary, Education student)

> *It's really hard for me and you know, the way they talk to each other and also because it's not just the language problem. Instead of planning lessons, giving lessons, teaching strategies, you need to also know things outside around school. I know the students find it hard to understand me because of my accent so I have been practising Aussie slang.* (Harry, Education student)

Another issue related to language was the specific vocabulary related to the professional work in which the students were immersed during work placement. For Sunil, a business student, the language related to accounting was sometimes confusing:

> *I haven't really had much experience in a company as big as this before. In [my home country] I worked in a small business that kept all its accounts on paper ledgers. We did have some computers but they didn't work that well. In this company I have to learn a lot more about what things are called and labelled etc.* (Sunil, Business student)

> *I was confused by terms commonly used in Australian schools that I didn't know such as calling the roll and put your hands up…I really needed to work on learning these terms. My supervisor was very helpful, she understood I was a student [teacher] and didn't know everything.* (Jamie, Education student)

In relation to how reflection looks and feels for international students with cultural and language differences, students were able to reflect at all levels to face challenges.

The volunteering participants were also able to highlight how sometimes their skills and difference benefitted the place where they helping out.

> *My host has been really lovely and asked me to help them out with their [home country] clients. Because they can't speak the language I was able to communicate effectively with these clients which, my host, said brought them more money. I felt really good about myself then.* (Lily, Business student)

Areas or lack of support

The international students often indicated that they found it hard to know where to find support in Australia. In another study we found that effective communication was a major contributing factor to international students' success in work placement. Even though international students knew about support mechanisms at university they often did not utilize them when on work placement.

One student mentioned they always wanted to call their family or friends back home but the time difference was not convenient. It meant that she had to stay up into the early morning hours if she needed help and then wake up early to go to work placement. This put more pressure on her, being tired all the time.

In Speech Pathology the students noted how important it was for them to be able to talk to each other. This occurred whether they were in the same work context or different work places. They had scheduled a regular weekly catch up so that they were able to reflect on their time and offer each other support if needed.

In relation to host supervisors the international students had mixed experiences. Some students were very upset about their experiences and said their host supervisors were very unsupportive. William, an education student, *reported* that his first mentor teacher would *"just let them get away with it. Students would say to each other and the teacher, "Shut up c***" and then the teacher would say, "Okay, I don't care".* For William this was distressing, and he related and reasoned that: *"Maybe that is [the school's] culture, but you can't expect us [pre-service teachers] to control and respect guys like that…I grew up in a culture where this would not be allowed or tolerated"*.

In William's second placement however, he noted a strongly different situation:

> *My mentor teacher really understands me and helps me a lot… she doesn't judge me in terms of my English language but helps me to get my grammar and spelling right" and "For me it is difficult to think of the terms, say for Renaissance music, in English—sometimes these words don't exist in Chinese… I have to work hard at this and my teacher and my university lecturer really helps me.* (William, Education student)

For Danielle, a psychology student, a similar experience occurred. Her first supervisor was *'very unsupportive'*.

She said that:

> *my written skill was, according to him, not up to the standard of what he expected, so when he actually read my report he was furious to find like grammar typos… he was just like "[Danielle], this is not my job to actually correct your grammar you have to deal with that". He made a huge deal about it, and then it's not even like it's not even the content of the report itself it's just the fact that he kind of found typo here and there.*

Danielle was able to accept that she needed to work on her written communication but with her second supervisor more support was provided. Her supervisor indicated for her to not worry too much and that they would provide assistance with editing. This made Danielle feel part of the team.

> *[T]he one thing that actually find really helpful is to give me autonomy but also offer some support as well when I need, so I think I feel I think I learn more when I feel challenged but supported at the same time. In this clinical placement I felt more like a valued member of the team, not just a student from uni.*

By the end of their study programs the international students were able to articulate more clearly how their work place experiences benefited them as a professional. They were also more reflective about how supervisors and other staff or support people around them should also offer a more empathetic approach to international students, given the distinct challenges they faced.

> *Stand in my shoes and think about my problem, to think about how I feel as an international student and also a new pre-service teacher.* (Shen, Education student)

> *I learn from my mistakes. I always try to ask my supervisor how I can improve but sometimes that has been hard. Some supervisors are really supportive and practice with me. One even told me to practice in front of a mirror but then there was one who only told me I was wrong but didn't say how I can be better. I'm trying to be a reflective teacher…just trying to be the best teacher I can.* (Penny, Education student)
> *I consider myself to be a rather polite person so I didn't even have to disagree with them so I needed to only write down their answers and also I was listening…I was just listening and that's kind of the main strategy, just to listen quietly and ask some guided questions to learn more. I am always learning.* (Alena, Business student)

REFLEXIVITY AND EMPLOYABILITY

In formal education, students are generally required to demonstrate their mastery of knowledge in a way that can be graded and compared. Assessment thus relies on certainty – making a case for what you know. Reflective processes, on the other hand, thrive on uncertainty and doubt (Boud, 1999; Ryan, 2015). What is it I don't know? What are the factors that might be affecting my performance? Will this course of action work? Am I invested enough to make an effort? Who else is impacted by my decisions? Workplaces mostly require skills in negotiating the latter – uncertainty – and responding with 'in-the-moment' problem solving, levels of risk-taking and innovative solutions. In preparing students for contemporary learning and professional contexts, where digital disruption promotes rapid change, it is important for higher education experiences to be imbued with speculative reflective processes. The use of critical incidents (McAllister et al., 2006), for example, is a generative way to develop international students' reflective and intercultural competencies, particularly in work places.

When students are able to draw on new repertoires and skills to inform their deliberations and to take action that produces benefits for self and others, they are more prepared for changing work places. Importantly, for learning to produce ongoing benefits for both the learner and their work or study environment, it must involve reflexivity as a necessary condition of active engagement. Mere exposure to content fails to instill a form of learning that prepares individuals for a world where knowledge and skills must be constantly evaluated, analyzed and revised for the demands of uncertain situations (McGuire, Lay, & Peters, 2009). Reflexive learning processes (Archer, 2012; Grossman, 2008) include: (i) recognizing issues or critical instances (McAllister et al., 2006); (ii) reflecting on one's capabilities and desires in relation to the issue; (iii) weighing up contributing social structures; (iv) thinking creatively and critically about the issue (Barton & Ryan, 2014); (v) making informed decisions; and (vi) taking appropriate action. These processes can be made visible and can be modelled and practiced at university to enhance students' reflective thinking and reflexive capabilities. These capabilities can be supported in different ways to suit different students, different contexts and different purposes.

CONCLUDING THOUGHTS

Throughout this paper we have identified the need for higher educators to consider how reflection, reflective thinking and reflexivity might be different for international students given their prior experience in their home countries and other contexts. We argued that reflection is important in making sense of oneself in relation to others as well as contexts in which we study and work. It is also integral for us to be able to reimagine or plan personal, professional and social experience whereby all may benefit. Considering reflection for and with international students has potential for their domestic counterparts, higher education staff and others to further understand what international students may face during their time as a student overseas.

Our research has shown that international students are able to work through all levels of reflection from reporting, relating, reasoning and reconstructing when they face positive environments in the workplace. However, students tended to only report and reason when things were not going so well. This could mean that international students' ability to reflect clearly and deeply when stressed was inhibited. We do acknowledge this could also be the case for domestic students so further research could include a comparative study between international and domestic students.

It is clear that international students face distinct challenges, particularly in relation to work placements and that regular reflection is required to ensure success. Rodgers' framework as well as Archer's concept of reflexivity both provide an effective way to consider how we, as higher educators, might support international students during their study. The literature reveals that international students often aim to work in countries other than their own, so ongoing reflection is critical in meeting this goal.

REFERENCES

Archer, M. (2000). *Being human: The problem of agency*. Cambridge: Cambridge University Press.

Archer, M. (2012). *The reflexive imperative in late modernity*. Cambridge: Cambridge University Press.

Bain, J. D., Ballantyne, R., Mills, C., & Lester, N.C. (2002). *Reflecting on practice: Student teachers' perspectives*. Flaxton: Post Pressed.

Barton, G. & Ryan, M. (2014). Multimodal approaches to reflective teaching and assessment in higher education. *Higher Education Research & Development.* 33(3), 409-424.

Barton, G. M., Hartwig, K., Bennett, D., Cain, M., Campbell, M., Ferns, S., Jones, L., Joseph, D., Kavanagh, M., Kelly, A., Larkin, I., O'Connor, E., Podorova, A., Tangen, D., & Westerveld, M. (2017). Work placement for international students: A model of effective practice. In G. M. Barton & K. Hartwig (Eds.), *Professional Learning in the Work Place for International Students: Exploring Theory and Practice,* (pp. 13-34). Switzerland: Springer Publishers.

Barton, G. M. & Ryan, M. (2017). Reflection and reflective practice for international students and their supervisors in context. In Barton, G. & Hartwig, K. (Eds), *Professional learning in the work place for international students: Exploring theory and practice.* Basel: Springer. 93-110.

Boud, D. (1999). Avoiding the traps/ seeking good practice in the use of self assessment and reflection in professional courses. *Social Work Education, 18*(2), 121-132.

Braun, V., & Clarke, V. (2006). Using thematic analysis in psychology. *Qualitative Research in Psychology, 3,* 77-101. http://dx.doi.org/10.1191/1478088706qp063oa

Chinn, C., Buckland, L., & Samarapungavan, A. (2011). Expanding dimensions of epistemic cognition: Arguments from philosophy and psychology. *Educational Psychologist, 46*(3), 141–167. https://doi.org/10.1080/00461520.2011.587722

de Schepper, J., & Sotiriadou, P. (2018). A framework for critical reflection in sport management education and graduate employability. *Annals of Leisure Research, 21*(2), 227-245.

Dewey, J. (1933). *How we think.* Buffalo, New York: Prometheus Books. Original edition, 1910.

Freebody, P., C. Maton, and J. R. Martin. 2008. Talk, text, and knowledge in cumulative, integrated learning: A response to 'intellectual challenge'. *Australian Journal of Language and Literacy* 31 (2):188-201.

Furman, R., Coyne, A., & Negi, N.J. (2008). An international experience for social work students: Self-reflection through poetry and jounral writing exercises. *Journal of Teaching in Social Work, 28*(1), 71-85.

Garrett, R. (2014). *Explaining international student satisfaction: Insights from the international student barometer.* Retrieved from: https://www.igraduate.org/assets/2014-Explaining-Satisfaction.pdf

Greene, J. A., & Yu, S. B. (2016). Educating critical thinkers: The role of epistemic cognition. *Policy Insights from the Behavioral and Brain Sciences, 3*(1), 45–53. https://doi.org/10.1177/2372732215622223

Grossman, R. (2008). Structures for facilitating student reflection. *College Teaching, 57*(1), 15-22.

Hunter, C., Pearson, D. & Gutierrez, A. R. (2015). Interculturalization and Teacher Education: Theory to Practice. New York: Routledge.

Khalili, H., Orchard, C., Spence Laschinger, H.K., & Farah, R. (2013). An interprofessional socialization framework for developing an interprofessional identity among health professions students. *Journal of Interprofessional Care, 27*(6), 448–453.

Kienhues, D., Feucht, F., Ryan, M. & Weinstock, M. (2017). Informed reflexivity: Enacting epistemic virtue. *Educational Psychologist*, 52(4), 284-298. http://dx.doi.org/10.1080/00461520.2017.1349662

Komins, B. J., & Nicholls, D. G. (2003). Cultivating critical self-reflection in an international context: The development of an American studies curriculum in Turkey. *College literature, 30*(3), 68-87.

Korthagen, F., & Vasalos, A. (2005). Levels in reflection: Core reflection as a means to enhance professional growth. *Teachers and Teaching: Theory and Practice, 11*(1), 47-71. https://doi.org/10.1080/1354060042000337093

Lunn, J. Ferguson, L. & Ryan. M. (2017). Changing epistemic cognition in the context of teaching and teacher education: A new conceptual framework for reflection and reflexivity. *Educational Psychologist.* http://dx.doi.org/10.1080/00461520.2017.1333430

McAllister, L., Whiteford, G., Hill, B., Thomas, N. & Fitzgerald, M. (2006). Reflection in intercutlural learning: Examining the international experience through a critical incident approach. *Reflective Practice, 7*(3), 367-381.

McGuire, L., Lay, J., & Peters, J. (2009). Pedagogy of reflective writing in professional education. *Journal of the Scholarship of Teaching and Learning, 9*(1), 93-107.

Mezirow, J. (2006). An overview of transformative learning. In P. Sutherland & J. Crowther (Eds.), *Lifelong Learning,* (pp. 90-105). London: Routledge.

Moje, E. (2008). Foregrounding the disciplines in secondary literacy teaching and learning: A call for change. *Journal of Adolescent and Adult Literacy 52*(2), 96-107.

Moon, J. A. (2013). *Reflection in learning and professional development: Theory and practice.* London: Routledge.

Rodgers, C. (2002). Seeing student learning: Teacher change and the role of reflection. *Harvard Educational Review, 72*(2), 230-253.

Ryan, M. (2013). The pedagogical balancing act: Teaching reflection in higher education. *Teaching in Higher Education. 18*(2), pp. 144-155.

Ryan, M. (2015). Reflective and reflexive approaches in higher education: A warrant for lifelong learning? In Ryan, M. E. (Ed), *Teaching Reflective Learning in Higher Education: A Systematic Approach Using Pedagogic Patterns,* (pp. 3-14). Sydney: Springer.

Ryan, M. E. & Ryan, M. C. (2015). A model for reflection in the pedagogic field of higher education. In Ryan, M. E. (Ed), *Teaching Reflective Learning in Higher Education: A Systematic Approach Using Pedagogic Patterns,* (pp. 15-30). Sydney: Springer.

Sadler, D. R. (2010). Beyond feedback: Developing student capability in complex appraisal. *Assessment & Evaluation in Higher Education, 35*(5), 535-550.

Schuldberg, J., Fox, N., Jones, C., Hunter, P., Bechard, M., Dornon, L., Gotler, S., Shouse, H., & Stratton, M. (2012). Same, same – but different: The development of cultural humility through an international volunteer experience. *International Journal of Humanities and Social Science, 2*(17), 17-30.

Starr-Glass, D. (2017). Troubling metaphors and international student adjustment: Reflections from a transnational place. *Journal of International Students, 7*(4): 1126-1134.

Taylor, S., Ryan, M., & Pearce, J. (2015). Enhanced student learning in accounting utilising web-based technology, peer-review feedback and reflective practices: a learning community approach to assessment. *Higher Education Research & Development, 34*(6), 1251-1269. DOI: 10.1080/07294360.2015.1024625.

Volet, S. (2004). Challenges of internationalisation: Enhancing intercultural competence and skills for critical reflection on the situated and non-neutral nature of knowledge. *Language and Academic Skills in Higher Education, 6*, 1-10.

BIOGRAPHIES

Georgina Barton, PhD, is a Professor and Associate Head – Research in the School of Education at the University of Southern Queensland, Brisbane, Australia. Before being an academic, Georgina taught in schools for over 20 years including teaching English in South India with Australian Volunteers International. Georgina also has extensive experience in teaching the arts in schools and universities and often utilizes the arts to support students' literacy learning outcomes. She has over 130 publications including as the lead editor of a book titled *Professional Learning for International Students: Exploring Theory and Practice.* She is a Principal Fellow of the Higher Education Academy in the UK. Email: georgina.barton@usq.edu.au

Mary Ryan, PhD, is Professor and Dean of Education at Macquarie University, Sydney, Australia. Her research is in the areas of teachers' work in, and preparation for, diverse classrooms, reflexive learning and practice, writing pedagogy and assessment and reflective writing. She led a highly successful Australian Learning and Teaching Council grant (2010/11) on reflective learning across disciplines in higher education. Her current Australian Research Council Discovery projects are in the areas of classroom writing and preparing reflexive teachers for diverse classrooms. She is a Principal Fellow of the Higher Education Academy in the UK. Email: mary.ryan@macquarie.edu.au

Peer-Reviewed Article
Special Edition | Reflection and Reflective Thinking

© *Journal of International Students*
Volume 10, Issue S2 (2020), pp. 17-35
ISSN: 2162-3104 (Print), 2166-3750 (Online)
ojed.org/jis

Creative Practice as a Catalyst for Developing Connectedness Capabilities: A Community Building Framework from the Teaching International Students Project

Kim Snepvangers
Arianne Rourke
University of New South Wales, Australia

ABSTRACT

Focusing on a section of the Teaching International Students (TIS) project this article captures student and mentor perspectives within a Project-Based Professional Experience (PBPE) in the context of a large research-intensive university in Sydney, Australia. Animations co-produced with students were part of a Work Integrated Learning (WIL) compulsory upper level course, leading to a 'Community Building Framework'. The research goal shifted the educational purpose from didactic physical placements to collaborative dynamics where students, including international students, staff, and industry perspectives were 'valued'. Prioritising intercultural learning 'challenged' contested attitudes and 'built' communities of practice in a workforce focused ecology. Findings emerged from reflective interchanges whilst working iteratively and collaboratively with students, to inform the PBPE online framework. Implications for WIL academic planning included: scope for asynchronous autonomous action beyond traditional ways of working; opportunities to model creative problem solving at scale; and critical thinking skills in transferability mode adaptable to future digital workplaces.

Keywords: Work Integrated Learning (WIL), International Students, creative practice, reflection, Problem Based Learning (PBL)

Research Focus

In a 2018 article written for the peak Work Integrated Learning (WIL) body, the Australian Collaborative Education Network (ACEN), Lomm, Snepvangers and Rourke argued, that for many international students seeking a creative industry WIL experience 'connectedness capabilities' (Bridgstock, 2016) can be difficult to achieve without greater institutional and policy support. To identify what kind of 'connected capabilities' are needed when international students embark on creative industry WIL experiences, a range of international policies and a proposal for a Community Building Framework was purposefully planned. The framework does not directly reference the terms 'connectedness' or 'connectivity': there is an implied relationship of professional and industry partnerships as an ecology that need to be nurtured through networked connections. This article reports on the values, challenges and events that were required to build a network of professional 'in country' connections as a Community Building Framework.

This framework is a curriculum planning scaffold situated within a university Problem Based Professional Experience (PBPE) context. This article reports on one specific outcome from a larger project known as the Teaching International Students (TIS) project. The authors are positioned in the research as industry mentors to reflect on shifts in student learning using an 'Ecologies of Practice' lens (Kemmis, Wilkinson, Edwards-Groves, Hardy, Grootenboer, & Bristol, 2014; Snepvangers & Rourke, 2018). In the role of 'insider-practitioners', as academic industry mentors we reflected on how Project-Based (PB) learning has been designed within a Professional Experience (PE) program situated in a large Australian university. The design of the PBPE adaptively transfers individual student media artwork and studio skills to a wider audience through a scaffolded, yet iterative networked ecology. Animations developed in the PBPE provide an example of creative practice where both international and domestic students work with academics to co-design 'visual learning artefacts' (VLA). The PBPE described in this article placed value on moving individual media practice towards a public facing professional pedagogy. This approach valued clustering of creative/communicative capabilities as rigorous ways of thinking and was actively planned to encourage diverse cultural perspectives and to challenge contested attitudes about WIL Mentors working with international students.

This article illustrates how the purposeful design of counter-dependent media artefacts (animations) act as "catalysts for conversation" (Snepvangers, Rourke, Myoung, Lin, & Cho, 2019, p. 12) in a meaning making reflective process (Rodgers, 2002). A rigorous 'Community Building Framework' has been designed to promote students' self-confidence, critical thinking skills and empowerment to self-manage change and prepare for real world workplace mobility. Dilemmas common to many students (domestic and international) in the tertiary setting, such as the first lecture, procrastination and group work act as 'catalysts for conversation' in situating the content of the animations. In this way, VLAs act as both staff and student resources to perpetuate new ecologies of creative practice. The research focused on how to develop connectedness capabilities in a co-design capacity that had actionable deliverables. The authors' hypothesised that these VLAs have the capacity to unite local and international students in a WIL Project and enculturate a self-generating system within and around students, which emphasised connectedness (Bridgstock, 2016) and meaning-making (Rodgers, 2002). The objective was to actively plan a PBPE creative practice framework to equip students with capacities for self-organised autonomous action post-graduation and to prioritise local and International students working together.

Research objective

The following hypothesis was proposed: PBPE is positively related to meaningful outcomes and connectedness capabilities related to international students' preparedness for work experience. A key focus is valuing the dynamics between individual students, academics and community/industry mentors within a workforce focused ecology.

LITERATURE REVIEW

Australian International Education Policies

Graduate employability in the International Education policy context in Australia is wide ranging and a full discussion is beyond the scope of this article. For the purposes of articulating how creative practice and project-based mentoring can act as catalysts for change, this article focuses on how the concept of connectedness is articulated in a select group of policies. In 2013, the International Education Advisory Council (IEAC), formed by the Australian Government, produced *Australia: Educating Globally* report. The report highlighted a number of economic and educational needs, constraints and challenges, specifically the significance of professional partnerships to enrich cultural understanding in workplace culture. Cultural understanding, educational quality and English Language Proficiency (ELP) were signalled as important in enhancing employability skills.

In 2016, the three-pillar strategy identified by the Australian government in the *National Strategy for International Education 2025* (NSIE) emphasized training and research for future skilling, employability and engaging with industry through WIL opportunities. Linking courses with industry in this policy was described using three pillars titled: *Strengthening the fundamentals*; *Making transformative partnerships* and *Competing Globally*. The second pillar is of most importance to this article, as the authors are interested in how ideas about collaboration engage with robust links to industry, innovation transfer, internships and work-based learning. In the strategy, enhancing connected graduate employability involves strengthening overseas government-to-government and institution-to-institution partnerships. Enhancing mobility supports the significance of having relevant and flexible visas for study and work for international students. The importance of networked connections through alumni partnerships, such as in the *Australian Global Alumni Engagement Strategy 2016-2020*, also supports this development. NSIE sets out best practice in making social, professional, cultural and alumni connections. As argued by Lomm, Snepvangers and Rourke (2018), policies demonstrate disparate references to connectedness and professional identity formation, which they see as key for professional success in host countries. When working with international students a reflective practice lens was used (Schön, 1983, 1987; Kemmis et.al, 2014) to reveal textual and visual evidence of students' 'lived experiences' using an 'ecologies of practice' lens (Kemmis, et al., 2014). The work of Bronfenbrenner in Zhang (2018) and the work of Snepvangers and Rourke (2018) and Rourke and Snepvangers (2016) provide structures for enhancing connectedness to address these gaps in current policy. The 'Community Building Framework' and events and deliverables from this project demonstrate how an individual psychological reading has been extended beyond family/home and individual creative practices, towards peer to peer and industry learning ecologies.

The 'Gig' Economy

The artistic project-based process mirrors many creative start-ups, 'gig' economies as well as co-design practices in the professional and commercial world. Here, virtual, mobile, digital platforms as well as a dual focus on sharing economies (Narasimhan, Papatla, et al., 2018) and outsourcing (Green, Walker, Alabulththim, Smith, Phillips, 2018) as a new way of working are increasingly the custom. In this more recent entrepreneurial ecology, individuals act as creators/sellers shifting the focus from professional business models towards ordinary consumers becoming prosumers, able to work, sell and create services and goods that were once only exclusively produced by larger enterprises. In the 'gig' economy, employees no longer work in long term 'jobs', rather they are hired for 'gigs', under malleable arrangements where they work to complete particular tasks within a defined timeframe (Friedman, 2014). Typically, loyalty does not extend beyond the life of the project, focus on real world issues or tend to engage with mobile media (Ma & Yang, 2018). The PBPE as discussed in this article, focuses on developing international students' academic and cognitive mobility and equipping them with self-confidence and maximum adaptability in the creative industries to move beyond a disciplinary focus towards interdisciplinary clusters of skills. In the case of the PBPE this included shifting animation and media arts students from a focus on being an animator with a Media Arts degree, towards presenting storyboards to clients, time-management technologies and ethics, participating in a range of professional presentational formats (workshops, prizes, forums, conferences etc.) and group learning with mentors and peers.

Linking Reflection and the World of Work

The ecological link the authors make, lies between practice and reflection in adult learning environments articulated by Glowacki-Dudka and Barnett (2007). The shift for these authors, is in the transformation from reflective practice as an individual pursuit towards reflection being a critically important factor when engaging with organizations and communities. In other words, when reflective practice was engaged with, for example, an industry group, collective concerns and expectations could be examined. A commitment to learning from experience and from evidence is the critical part of reflective practice, in contrast, learning 'recipes' for action or applying textbook knowledge to practice was less likely to result in students self-reflecting and gaining new insights and eventually autonomy (Ashcroft & Foreman-Peck, 1994). Korthagen (2001) defined reflection as the "mental process of trying to (re)structure an experience, a problem or existing knowledge or insights" (p.58). In order for this to eventuate, students need to go through the process of negotiating and finally agreeing to their own meaning of the term 'reflection' (Moon, 1999) and apply this understanding to their role and interactions with others. Internships and work placements can provide international students with the opportunity to develop their self-knowledge and individual professional behaviour (Eraut, 1994) in a foreign country workplace setting and provide opportunities through the reflective process to apply their university learning to a real-world context. As has been ascertained by Barton, Hartwig and Le (2018): "Findings showed that there is a need for universities to better support international students in completing reflective and self-evaluative assessment" (p.1). Reflection can also lead to professional development learning opportunities beyond a university setting that facilitate students to examine and evaluate what they do in a workplace environment and why they respond and behave in a particular way (Harvey & Knight, 1996).

Reflective Practice

Schön (1983, 1987) advocated that reflection is an important part of the learning process as reflectivity allows the student to see the fundamental relationship between their actions and their framing of the situation. For Moon (1999) reflection is "a tool that facilitates personal learning towards the outcome of personal development", that she argues "ultimately leads towards empowerment and emancipation" (p.88). The PBPE discussed in this article aimed to build international students' autonomy, self-confidence and empowerment to manage change in preparing for real world workplace mobility. Rodgers (2002) introduced four functions of reflection: 1) a meaning-making process, 2) a rigorous way of thinking, 3) being important in and for community, and 4) a set of attitudes. Reflection is an important part of the process of finding meaning and relevance in learning. In this 'meaning-making process' (Rodgers, 2002) students apply their own personal experience and understanding to their learning. Through this process students' identities, values, and behaviour patterns are related to how they participate, engage and contribute to the world they live in (Keeling, 2004). It is also essential for international students in higher education to develop 'rigorous way of thinking' (Rodgers, 2002), not just through the tertiary learning process but also through problem-solving activities in a professional work-related environment, a necessary skill if they are to acquire the attributes for global employability. For international students, reflecting through their creative professional practice experience provides them with the opportunity to express multiple points of view on issues that may be difficult to communicate verbally or in writing for non-English first language speakers (Snepvangers & Rourke, 2018).

International students in particular, need to feel that they are important in and valued by their host professional community (Rodgers, 2002), through having a positive experience in a foreign working environment they can feel empowered to manage change in preparing for real world workplace mobility as global citizens. Developing a set of attitudes (Rodgers, 2002) congenial to a professional environment requires international students to engage in supportive, fruitful relationships with internship hosts, employers and mentors. This is reciprocated by the vital link between the university environment, meaningful outcomes and future industry workplaces. According to the literature Project-Based Learning increases student motivation and enthusiasm for learning, facilitates a sense of community and enhances and deepens learning, resulting in an increase in graduate employability attributes, confidence, leadership and problem-solving skills (Bovill, Cook-Sather, & Felten, 2011; Fieldsend-Danks, 2016; Bell, 2010). One specific aspect of this research was to look at indications of confidence in their project-based learning through mentor reflections as a way of gauging students' connectedness and potential employability in the gig economy.

Project-Based Learning

The authors argue that online project-based experience is like a physical placement on site with a mentor, who organizes project-based experiences and learning around projects. Whilst project-based learning is not new, the key features summarized here from Thomas (2000) have salience for this work. Typically, projects are:

- complex tasks, based on challenging questions or problems, that involve students in design,
- problem-solving, decision making, or investigative activities;
- give students the opportunity to work relatively autonomously over extended periods of time;
- culminate in realistic products, technologies and presentations;
- comprise authentic content and assessment;
- engage cooperative learning, reflection, and incorporation of professional skills within a community of practice/inquiry.

In PBPE, typically, projects were facilitated by a mentor guiding and informing the project with explicit goals and milestones and supervised by the university PBPE Convenor. Clear structure of project check-ins with mentors was envisaged and project deliverables were agreed upon as well as a range of virtual WIL opportunities currently emerging. For PBPE, students complete 150 hours remotely as part of a 'Study from Home' model with some face to face (F2F) meetings and synchronous and asynchronous tasks. What was significant about PBPE is that in many contemporary WIL placements students were unable to work from home as typically they shadowed an industry mentor in a real world learning physical location. This initiative anticipates a stronger self-management and self-organisational suite of dispositions. Mirroring the 'gig' economy, without day to day physical placements, this approach fosters a scholarly approach to mentoring in a 'studying from home' mode. This research is well positioned to engage with future research directions that will embrace emergent Government directives, Work Integrated Learning (WIL), central and legal requirements to resolve arrangements for PBPE online.

PARTICIPANTS

The WIL academic course has an average of two-hundred students enrolled in the course each year. This study focuses on five final year art and design students (local n=3; international =2; of which 3 were female and 2 male) who self-selected the authors' PBPE project in 2018 and 2019. All of the students had graphic design skills and they had all previously produced animations during their university studies. The 'match-making' PBPE process comprises the following:

1) Industry mentors in collaboration with the Course Convenor writes project descriptions, skill requirements and provide their contact details, which were then posted online. In some instances, students write the projects.
2) Students choose a project from an online portal and email the PBPE mentor their curriculum vitae (CV); mentors pick the student that best matches their project requirements and organize a meeting.
3) Student and mentor meet to discuss project expectations, a decision is made as to the suitability of the match, if both parties agree to work together a PBPE contract is signed.
4) Once the project contract has been submitted to the online portal, checks on duty of care and due diligence were completed by the university Course Convenor.
5) Once approved the students start immediately on projects, at any time of the year.

RESEARCH DESIGN

To broaden the workplace opportunities for art and design students, academics were invited by the PBPE Convenor to propose projects that fit the PBPE objectives. This case study investigates the experiences of 5 students (2 in 2018 & 3 in 2019) mentored by the authors in their PBPE project over a two-year timeframe. This PBPE project provided students with the opportunity to plan and produce animations on topics of their choice that focused on the experiences of international students in higher education. The animations were presented as 'catalyst for conversation' in academic career development workshops, faculty and university-wide forums and National and International conferences. The PBPE students were provided with the opportunity to pitch their ideas in a professional setting, self-time manage the process of planning and production of their animations; adapt to working from home and working within a limited timeframe as well as experience various ways of presenting their work in a variety of educational contexts. The key innovative feature of the PBPE was that the work occurred within a university context to develop Visual Learning Artefacts (animations) in a 'Study from Home' mode. In this case the mentors were university academics (insider-practitioners) and rather than requiring the international and local students to attend a physical work placement, the Community Building Framework allowed for a series of planned meetings and events. Key dates for deliverables and outcomes were collectively decided and flexibly delivered to prioritise project-led workplace relationships in each phase in an emergent and iterative process.

METHOD

The authors report on the research using a reflective insider-practitioner perspective on the PBPE that scaffolds into a phased university course Work Integrated Learning (WIL) project. The framework developed by the authors, prioritized collaboration and real-world expectations. Through a reflection-on-action (Schön in Rodgers, 2002) process the authors proposed a PBPE Community-Building Framework (refer to *Table 1: Project Based Professional Experience (PBPE) – Mentor Guide)*, using a colour-coded system to identify key moments. The key was derived from the literature, including Ecologies of Practice (Kemmis, et. al., 2014), Project-Based Learning (Thomas, 2000) and Rodger's (2002) reflective terms, focusing on 'meaning-making'. Concepts proposed and synthesised by the authors centre on the project's key objectives of Valuing (V), Challenging (C), Building (B), which are colour-coded. The use of the word 'phase', rather than a weekly program of study, signals the iterative and temporal process of transformational and meaningful outcomes.

The key moments in the developing student/mentor/community ecologies were linked to a temporal process of moving through guided activities to develop the student's capacities to move from dependency, through counter-dependence towards the goal of independence and building student connectedness in the long term. The authors analytical process included identifying key objectives V, C and B in relation to their reflections at the completion of the project. Data was gathered from physical F2F observations, which were logged in a reflective practice journal after each phase of the project. Selected mentor 'insider-practitioners' quotes (authors as academic industry mentors) were then collected. Emergent themes were based on the recordings that best captured student learning in terms of confidence, shifts in understanding collaborative practice and a sense of themselves as a creative professional in each phase. The grey block text indicates a physical meeting with all participants (students/mentors/community) as a key idea in the authors' use of reflection as a tool in the methodology of this research. Data collection included mentor reflections (journals), student feedback surveys regarding pre-post PBPE and deliverables included: storyboards, animations and research posters. At the completion of their degree programs, permission was sought from students to include their reflections anonymously from the completed WIL course – university ethics approval number HC190925.

Alongside creative practice students, the authors tracked monthly emergent student-led tasks, deliverables and outcomes to show gradual intercultural flows towards connectedness, captured in Table 1. The events, students' roles, scope and purpose of each event were compiled for future research. No pre-determined plan or step-by-step procedure was imposed at the beginning of the PBPE rather, the authors reflected on how to build a student-led ecosystem progressively that evolves and values both individual and student group issues and concerns. This methodology iteratively captures new data about how to work using temporal learning modes and trust-building beyond physical placements. A qualitative lens was used for this research with each of the five student animation projects conceived as one case study to provide real-world applicability.

Scope of the Project

Meetings with the PBPE students and the mentors (both virtually and F2F were held at various points during the 10 phase WIL timeframe (Refer to Table 1: PBPE Mentor Guide below). Students were required to log their working at home hours on a timesheet and prepare 'work in progress' presentations at key times during the PBPE timeframe. At the first meeting students' brain-stormed ideas for their animations focusing on topics related to the international students' experience. The PBPE students based their animations on their own experiences, the local students talked to their international student cohort to form an idea for their animations. The PBPE students identified the following topics for their animations: group dynamics in the classroom - mixing the student cohort of international and local students; the importance of time management; working together on a common goal; presentation anxiety and first day introduction anxiety.

One of the main objectives for producing these 'Visual Learning Artifacts' was to use them as a catalyst for promoting conversations about challenging and contested attitudes about international students in the classroom. This creative medium assisted in promoting open conversations about classroom issues between students and students, teachers and teachers and between students and teachers. The animations were approximately five minutes in length and students were encouraged to use their own artistic style of representation. Students produced a series of storyboards to plan out each scene in their animations. These were discussed at virtual and F2F meetings where PBPE students and mentors provided constructive criticism of the animations before the final work was produced. The PBPE 'Community Building Framework' utilises creative ecologies and communicative capabilities already identified as meaningful outcomes from the research. Table 1 presents a Mentor Guide showing how students can move from individual concerns to a community focus entailing: Valuing Intercultural Learning, Challenging Mentoring/Career Development and Building Communities of Practice.

Key to Table 1: Project Objectives as applied in the Mentor Guide:

Table 1: Project-Based Professional Experience (PBPE)
Community Building Framework – Mentor Guide.

Temporal Iterative Transformation	F2F and/or online commitment	Tasks and Visual Learning Artefacts (VLA)
Led by Mentors(*Dependent) *Providing the meaning-making (Rodgers, 2002).*	**Phase 1** **Mentor Check-in**	* Introductions & Project Briefing. * Work Health & Safety induction to 'Study from Home' mode; work-flows; reporting; Students & mentor's role. * Discuss how to work effectively in F2F & online team/s. * Understanding the project phases; setting out components; timelines; deliverables & discussing technology requirements. V - Ice-break me activities to bring forth their own issues & concerns (what matters to each person in the intercultural classroom). C - Getting the most from your mentors, discussion about format of project - based meetings, emails, requirements, protocols. B - Moving from individual making practice to group meaning making.
	Phase 2	* User-centred design (as applicable). * Market research with people, target audiences. * Stakeholder-centred co-design in complex systems. V - Student perspectives on issues & concerns and mentor discuss what matters to the group in the intercultural classroom & discuss target audience. C - Design sprint or challenge - introduce to community. B - Sharing reflections and shifting ideas from personal psycho-social concerns, students feeling more confident in their interactions with others.
Co-Led by Students & Mentors (*Counter-dependent *Independent) *Collaborative meaning-making (Rodgers, 2002).*	**Phase 3** **Mentor Check-in** **Phase 3/4**	* Formative review of deliverables, review prototype development. * Principles to address industry challenges, rapid prototyping; lean design; concept catalogue creation; iterative co-design with industry. V - Group contributions & appreciating the input and opinions of others. C – Challenging existing beliefs about studio as a lone practice – sharing reflections & group decision making. Encouraging shared ideas to counter avoidance of asking questions and contributing.

		B – Moving from individual making practice to a group dynamic – discussion, bouncing around ideas & selection of one animation storyboard to promote critical thinking of individual practice. Demonstrating confidence in student interactions with mentors.
	Phase 4	* Prototype development – send samples as appropriate to mentor. * Take two photos of yourself "Studying from Home".
Transformative – meaning-making (Rodgers, 2002). Moving between phases.	**Phase 5**	* From storyboard prototype to demonstration of animation – public display; reception and trouble shooting. * Value propositions & business planning; mentor's shares pathways into practice. * Mentor's pitch training or other collaborative opportunity
	Phase 6 **Mentor Check-in**	* Summative review of deliverables. * Pitching, & industry showcase. planning. * Independent relationships – working on individual contribution; & self-initiated communication within the student group to complete collaborative project. V – Diverse student perspectives were seen in the context of the overall project success (how their contribution to JIS has a wider impact) C – How to work on another person's animation (conceptual & technical help – working as an organised team). B – public profile development; moving towards self-management of professional footprint. Students demonstrating confidence in their abilities as a creative professional
Led by Student (*Self-Generating Connectedness) Students' meaning-making (Rodgers, 2002).	**Phases 7-10** **Final Mentor Check-in**	* Prepare presentations (workshops, forums, conference presentations). * Address final component of completing animation; adding university branding. * Attend virtual debrief & F2F check in with mentor/s – sign off; Mentor Feedback Form; Timesheet & Project Profile. V- Self generated autonomous action; co-design format; C- Organisational Connectedness check. B - Students initiate and work as a cohesive and supportive group with students, academics, industry, & community to complete the PBPF project. Students are confident about seeking employment as a creative professional post university

V – **VALUING** Intercultural Learning - Valuing diverse cultural perspectives, co-design with international and domestic students alongside mentors as insider-practitioners;
C – **CHALLENGING** Mentoring/Career Development - Challenging contested attitudes and traditional ways of working through creative and reflective means over a defined project timeline;
B – **BUILDING** Communities of Practice - Building a community framework to promote student self-confidence, critical thinking and empower students to self-manage change and prepare for real-world workplace mobility

RESULTS

Students' reflections (pre and post) were recorded at the end of their PBPE. The authors' analysis of the reflective process acknowledged that often the best time to capture data regarding 'meaning-making' (Rodgers, 2002) was at the completion of the experience. Often when undergoing an experience, it can be difficult to see what has been achieved. The process mirrors the reflection-on-action cycle outlined by Schön in Rodgers (2002) whereby "the process is purposefully slowed down" (p.234) and in this case reflection is focused on academics as teachers reflecting on their role as mentors in an industry placement arrangement. The storyboards, animations and posters (See Table 1) and the presentation of these deliverables at events inform the following collected themes in the data. The three themes identified by the authors relate to what professional attributes the students, mentor and deliverables (events, posters, animations, interactions) revealed through the process of reflection. The first theme of 'developing confidence' relates to how students' progress through the PBPE from dependent (led by mentors) to counter-dependent (co-design) to interdependent self-generating connectedness (led by students). Evidence of students assuming control, taking initiative, developing confidence and self-motivation capabilities emerged from mentor and two student quotes as follows:

> The more we reassured students that it was not a case of 'me and my shadow' instead they would set their own pace and direction, the more self-confident they became during the PBPE *(Mentor One-Phase 3).*

> When I began PBPE, I was expecting less control and assumed I would take on the role as someone who would just follow others' creative direction. After working in a professional environment, I now know it is okay to offer up my own ideas and to take initiative in creative projects when it is necessary *(Participant 2).*

> You could see how intently each student listened and how they smiled at us as we engaged them in the project and encouraged them to feel that they had ownership of the process and that we were going to have fun working together *(Mentor Two-Phase).*

These reflections demonstrate how the students became more self-motivated and confident in their abilities as they progressed through the collaborative co-design process with their mentors. One student was particularly pleased to see how their scholarly knowledge and design practice skills, developed during their undergraduate studies, could be utilised in a 'real-world' working environment. Student and mentor reflected:

> Pre-PBPE, I was very anxious about the media arts industry and what sort of content would be considered industry grade, however after

> doing my PBPE, I feel more confident about my capabilities and what I can provide *(Participant 1)*.

> It was amazing to watch their confidence grow as they realised how much academics valued their creative outputs, many asking if they could use their animations in their teaching *(Mentor Two-Phase 10)*.

This student's reflection emphasizes their need to feel "being important in and for (a) community" (Rodgers, 2002), which is an important factor in the process of becoming a 'valued' creative professional. The second theme relates to 'developing creative ecologies' and making tacit professional skills and communicative capabilities visible as meaningful outcomes of the PBPE. Evidence of ecological thinking was demonstrated:

> Prior to this project, I mostly worked independently on personal projects in art and animation - this required a lot of self-reflection and lack of guidance when completing a production from start to finish *(Participant 3)*.

> The students valued the collaborative approach relying less on our judgements as mentors to reassure them that they were progressing instead they became more enthusiastic about the project, self-motivated and more secure in their ability to produce a professional outcome *(Mentor Two-Phase 5)*.

> The students by the end of the PBPE could articulate clearly their work's intention and pitch their ideas to all levels of the university hierarchy *(Mentor observation of students presenting at Poster Presentation-Phase 10)*.

The third theme regarding 'critical thinking skills' overlaps with valuing the role collaboration plays in developing creative practice into an ecology. Through the timeframe of the project students further developed their critical thinking skills as they worked through the stages of the design process from initial ideas to the final production and presentation of their creative outputs. As two of the students and a mentor reflected:

> When I was working as an undergraduate on assignments there was always a brief to follow, this project gave me the opportunity to think more critically about my practice, with a client in mind *(Participant 4)*.

> In particular, for this PBPE I tried a new animation style with limited time, and it worked out quite well, so it gave me a stronger sense of accomplishment *(Participant 1)*.

> Students needed reassurance at the beginning that there were no right or wrong approaches to the project and that all opinions and ideas were valued, once they could see we were sincere about this I could see how physically each student relaxed and became 'chatty' and excited to contribute ideas, critically think and talk over each other to get their opinions heard *(Mentor One-Phase 2).*

This evidence captures students moving from individual concerns where they often lacked confidence in their studio projects to thinking about their reception and audiences in the professional practice environment. Based on 'insider-practitioner' observations in the case of international students, this included shifting from a reluctance to engage and initiate to the insertion of their own understandings of creative practice as they moved on in their confidence as creative practitioner. The sense of achievement, empowerment, ability to work with others and development of leadership skills were also attributes developed during the PBPE:

> On completion of the PBPE I now feel empowered to start new projects with other people, and not just respond to an assignment brief *(Participant 5).*

> Pre-PBPE I was unsure what I wanted to do with my future and my degree, but I think the experience helped me to orientate my goals and what I want in terms of my career and future prospects *(Participant 1).*

> My practice has shifted in that working on this project with other creative professionals allowed for a more collaborative approach *(Participant 3).*

> Students were more self-assured about their problem-solving skills and ability to be pro-active and productive while working on projects both independently and collaboratively *(Mentor One -Phase 6).*

The key objectives of the PBPE were to build a community framework to empower students to self-manage change and prepare for real world workplace mobility and lifelong learning. The novel approach was exemplified: in this quote: *"Students were excited (animated faces) about taking a novel approach and having freedom to guide the projects outcome. One student expressed that it was important to them that they had ownership of the process and freedom to express their opinion without being graded or judged" (Mentor Two-Phase 4).* In terms of overall feelings of accomplishment, one student commented: *"This project evoked a new desire of mine: to create work that can be used to educate and inform viewers of issues and ideas that can improve our way of living" (Participant 2).* The PBPE students had 'real-world' work experiences such as completing time management software scheduling and participating in online and F2F work meetings, preparing and co-presenting in workshops and producing and presenting animations to be shown on different platforms for different audiences.

In this work situation the PBPE students demonstrated their adaptability and problem-solving skills while building on their capacity to work collaboratively and manage change. *"The students spoke up more as the meetings progressed, towards the end of the PBPE. I could see each student brimming with observations about how people had reacted positively to their work at workshops"* (Mentor One-Phase 7). Students' PBPE outputs included: time sheets, process diaries, story-boards, animations, workshop presentations, posters and CV development. One student reflected: *"PBPE helped greatly in conceptualising and improving the quality of my work in a professional context"* (Participant 3). By showing the animations at national and international conferences they received high-level exposure of their work to a wider public, which added to their CV and built their reputation as a creative practitioner. Working in partnership invites students to share in the responsibility of shaping their learning and teaching environment and therefore helps us to challenge the unhelpful positioning of students as 'consumers' (Felton et. al., 2013, p. 64).

DISCUSSION

Through developing this 'Community Building Framework' using a reflection-on-action methodology, the authors' have shown how to plan an academic creative practice WIL program for mentors. Table 1 was written at the completion of a two-year phased WIL program of study, working with international and local students in the Australian higher education context. Working iteratively across dependent, through counter-dependent then independent actionable tasks and deliverables, an initial finding concerned the importance of building quality partnerships. For example, evidence of valuing international student perspectives in the creative development of storyboards reflected personal concerns about studying in an Australian university. Each students'animations were valued as individual artistic pieces. Through identifying shared themes in their animations, students valued each other's contributions in ways that were not always possible within their usual undergraduate studies. Simultaneously, each person was challenged in the counter-dependent phases of the project through thinking about which individual contribution would best capture the group's key aim. Each student contributed to the construction of the final animation in a vicarious, yet valued way.

In terms of a second policy concern from the literature regarding the importance of networked connections, the authors purposely met F2F with all of the group members in a supportive scheduled set of meetings, (see grey blocked text in Table 1). This actively encouraged collaboration, initially mentor led, then through the co-design process, a student-led partnership emerged. Students gained confidence and their range of experiences in working as a team increased. The purposeful local and international student interactions in each planned phase, were a positive WIL outcome. Student and mentor data from finding number one, showed increased confidence resulting from meaningful engagement with novel processes in PBPE. Gradually, through increased individual, group, team and university presentational modes, enhanced creative ecologies were built as seen in finding number two, where creative contributions to the value chain were noted by students and academic mentors.

The third finding, regarding the significance of developing critical thinking skills, was a key aim of the 'Community Building Framework', to *Value, Challenge* and *Build* mentor and students' understanding of international student perspectives on project-based PBPE. This new iterative way of working in a 'Studying from Home' mode mimicked the 'gig' economy and future workplaces in an authentic way, as students devised projects in an asynchronous mode, rather than having pre-determined line managed jobs or tasks that were linear in both process and delivery. The authors were interested in mentorship as a dynamic organic collaboration beyond teacher/student, manager/managed, employer/employee relationship binaries. In this way the project deliverables allowed students the flexibility to work, sell and create services in a mobile way across a defined timeframe. By capturing ways of valuing engagement in a 'Community Building Framework', new communities of practice beyond one workplace, broke down hierarchies to extend networks and communities in newly evolving creative projects at scale. Key findings were the significance of achieving greater scope for asynchronous action beyond traditional ways of working; increased opportunities to model creative problem solving through a critical level of experience that led to further self-generating activities at scale; and finally situating critical thinking skills in a fluid and transferable mode adaptable to future digital workplaces.

Through the methodology of reflection, the authors' mapped the various events, as moments over time that enculturated graduate connectedness capabilities. Through planned, serendipitous as well as emergent activities, students increased their confidence and the adaptability of their creative practice from disciplinary dependency towards contributions to clusters of new ways of working in the gig economy, as captured in the student and mentor quotes. Students moved from being lone isolated practitioners to a newly discovered consciousness of the contribution that they could make to society and the workforce as they positioned themselves in an evolving public context as global citizens. This is evidenced by the fact that students could contribute to workshop conversations, provide insight into dilemmas in learning and present with assurance at various events with often high-profile academic communities. Working through identified themes in their PBPE creative practice (animations) such as first day anxiety, the findings extend confidence building capabilities beyond the course/program objectives to real-world contexts outside of university studies. The creative animations are mechanization resistant as they stem from authentic international student concerns, having all been distilled from 'catalysts for conversation' in a dialogic process over time. Simultaneously, the deliverables utilize a unique creative animation style, evolved from an individual student's studio artwork, yet also capture dilemmas that resonate with professional issues across disciplinary borders such as the first lecture, procrastination and group work.

The appeal lies in the personalized style of the animations, using relatable avatars that could be used by tutors across WIL courses as well as courses that valued the perspective of international students. The many requests for access to the animations for use in tertiary classrooms, provides further evidence of the efficacy of this creative approach. The number of people impacted as well as the range of accepted opportunities signals how students moved beyond being nervous about presenting to peers in a classroom or being unable to initiate activities when faced with new projects in culturally diverse industry contexts.

This work is innovative as creative (WIL) professional experiences typically occur in a physical location, working with a mentor on a day by day basis. PBPE has facilitated two modes of reflective reporting: one where students reflect on the shifts in their professional practice in project management beyond individual making practice towards collaborative practice with a client in mind. Secondly, for the authors the creation of an academic program of study that can signal the significance of iteration, without students having to be immersed in a physical site, each and every day. The emphasis was not on assessment in the same way as a typical course requirement but on authentic real-world experience across temporal iterative phases of transformation. The quotes and PBPE activities outlined in Table 1 demonstrate how the key objectives: **Valuing** Intercultural Learning, **Challenging** Mentoring/Career Development and **Building** Communities of Practice can evolve in the tertiary context. The PBPE students through these activities were able to reflect on the process, become more confident presenting their work, build on their CV's and widen their future work opportunities.

REFERENCES

Ashcroft, K. & Foreman-Peck, L. (1994). *Managing teaching and learning in Further and Higher Education.* Flamer.

Australian Government. (2016). *National strategy for international education 2025.* Canberra Department of Education and Training.

Barton, G. M., Hartwig, K., & Le, A. (2018). International students' perceptions of workplace experiences in Australian study programs: A Large-Scale Survey. *Journal of Studies in International Education, 23*(2), 248-264. DOI: 10.1177/1028315318786446

Bell, S. (2010). Project-based learning for the 21st century: Skills for the future. *The Clearing House: A Journal of Educational Strategies, Issues and Ideas, 83*(2), 39-43.

Bovill, C., Cook-Sather, A., & Felten, P. (2011). Students as co-creators of teaching approaches, course design and curricula: Implications for academic developers. *International Journal for Academic Development 16*(2): 133–145.

Bridgstock, R. (2016). *Graduate employability 2.0: Social networks for learning, career development and innovation in the digital age.* Discussion Paper. Retrieved from [http://www.graduateemployability2-0.com].

Eraut, M. (1994). *Developing professional knowledge and competence.* Falmer.

Felton, P. Bagg, J., Bumbry, M., Hill J., Hornsby, K., Pratt, M., & Weller, S. (2013). A call for expanding inclusive student engagement in SoTL. *Teaching and Learning Inquiry, 1*(2), 63–74.

Fieldsend-Danks, P. (2016). The dialogues project: Students as partners in developing research-engaged learning'. *Art, Design & Communication in Higher Education, 15*(1), 89-102.

Friedman, G. (2014). Workers without employers: shadow corporations and the rise of the gig economy. *Review of Keynesian Economics, 2*(2), 171–188.

Glowacki-Dudka, M., & Barnett, N. (2007). Connecting critical reflection and group development in online adult education classrooms, *International Journal of Teaching and Learning in Higher Education, 19*(1), 43-52.

Green, D. D., Walker, C., Alabulththim, A., Smith, D., Phillips, M. (2018). Fueling the gig economy: A case study evaluation of upwork.com. *Management and Economics Research Journal 4,* 104–112.

Harvey, L., & Knight, P. (1996). *Transforming higher education.* SRHE/Open University Press.

International Education Advisory Council (IEAC). (2013). *Australia: Educating globally.* Australian Government.

Keeling, R. (2004). *Learning reconsidered: A campus-wide focus on the student experience.* USA: NASPA.

Kemmis, S., Wilkinson, J., Edwards-Groves, C., Hardy, I., Grootenboer, P. & Bristol, L. (2014). *Changing practices, changing education.* Springer.

Korthagen, F. A. J. (2001). *Linking practice and theory: The pedagogy of realistic teaching education.* Lawrence Erlbaum.

Lomm, M., Snepvangers, K., & Rourke, A. (2018). *Connectedness in graduate employability: An investigation of current international education policies and relevant literature.* In J. Smith, K. Robinson & M. Campbell (Eds.), 7th National Australian Collaborative Network (ACEN) Conference Proceedings (pp. 80-84). Work Integrated Learning (WIL) Creating Connections: Building Futures, 3-5 October, Brisbane, Australia.

Ma, X., & Yang, S. (2018). Airtasker and the Australian freelance workers: The reflections on the gig economy. *International Journal of Advanced and Applied Sciences, 5*(7), 35-45.

Moon, J. (1999). *Reflection in learning and professional development: Theory and practice.* Kogan Page & Sterling, Stylus.

Narasimhan, C., Papatla, P., Jiang, B. Kopalle, P.K., Messinger, P.R., Moorthy, S., Proserpio, D., Subramanian, U., Wu, C., & Zhu, T. (2018). Sharing economy: Review of current research and future directions. *Customer Needs and Solutions, 5,* 93–106.

Rodgers, C. (2002). Seeing student learning: Teacher change and the role of reflection. *Harvard Educational Review, 72*(2), 230-253.

Rourke, A., & Snepvangers, K. (2016). Ecologies of practice in tertiary art & design: A review of two cases. *Higher Education, Skills and Work-Based Learning, Emerald Insight, 6*(1), 69-85.

Schön, D. A. (1983). *The reflective practitioner.* Jossey-Bass.

Schön, D. A. (1987). *Educating the reflective practitioner.* Jossey-Bass.

Snepvangers, K., Rourke, A., Myoung, G., Lin, S. & Cho, H. J. (2019). Shifting landscapes of international education: New conceptions of creativity as collaboration and partnerships. *Poster eBooklet: Embracing Change: Creating Opportunities.* In C. Ryan, A. Petanec, Z, Rushton & D. Wierzbica (Eds.), Pro Vice-Chancellor (Education) Portfolio, UNSW.

Snepvangers, K., & Rourke, A. (2018). Developing work-integrated learning with creative professionals in art, design and media: International students, online public profiles and sustainability. In A. Rourke, V. Rees, & G. Forsyth (Eds.), *Beyond graduate attributes: Embedding work integrated learning into undergraduate degrees* (pp. 73-95). Common Ground.

Thomas, J. W. (2000). *A review of research on project-based learning.* Retrieved from [http://www.autodesk.com/foundation].

Zhang, Y. L. (2018). Using Bronfenbrenner's ecological approach to understand academic advising with international community college students. *Journal of International Students, 8*(4), 1764–1782.

BIOGRAPHIES

Kim Snepvangers, PhD, is an Associate Professor at UNSW Faculty of Art & Design and a Scientia Education Academy (SEA) Fellow. Kim is also a Senior Fellow of the Higher Education Academy (SFHEA), and an award-winning educational leader in arts-based educational leadership research, Work Integrated Learning (WIL) and professional practice in creative ecologies. In 2018 she won an Australian Award for University Teaching (AAUT) Citation for 'Outstanding Contribution to Student Learning' and the inaugural International Society for Education through Art (InSEA) Award for Excellence in Research in Education through Art (AEREtA). Email: k.snepvangers@unsw.edu.au

Arianne Jennifer Rourke, EdD, is an Associate Professor at The University of New South Wales, Sydney, Faculty of Art & Design, she is a Fellow of the UNSW Scientia Education Academy (SEA). Arianne is also Senior Fellow of the Higher Education Academy (SFHEA) and contributes her expertise on the editorial boards of six International education journals. Her research is in higher education visual pedagogies and professional practices. Recently she co-curated with Dr Vaughan Rees, an 8-book series titled: 'Transformative Pedagogy in the Visual Domain', published by Common Ground Research Networks that received the 2018 Publisher's Award of Excellence. Email: A.Rourke@unsw.edu.au

Peer-Reviewed Article
Special Edition | Reflection and Reflective Thinking

© *Journal of International Students*
Volume 10, Issue S2 (2020), pp. 36-50
ISSN: 2162-3104 (Print), 2166-3750 (Online)
ojed.org/jis

Reflections of Learning Experiences of International Students in Sweden

Liisa Uusimaki
University of Gothenburg, Sweden

Susanne Garvis
Swinburne University, Australia

ABSTRACT

The purpose of this article is to present a qualitative study exploring a small cohort of nine international students' in-depth reflections about their teaching and learning experiences studying at a major Swedish University. Interestingly while there have been numerous studies reporting on the experiences of international students attending Anglo-Saxon universities, few studies have explored teaching and learning experiences of international students studying in Sweden. Using Carol Rodgers (2002) model of four functions of reflections provided a novel way to explore international students' reflections about their learning experiences in Sweden, especially how these are shown in the following different cycles, of presence, description, analysis and experimentation. Making sense of international students' experiences allows us as university lecturers to enhance our understanding how to better support international students' in their learning away from their home universities. A qualitative content analysis was employed to the data collected from 3 focus groups. Findings showed that the international students experienced several cultural and contextual differences from that of their home universities. The differences related to course structures, teaching and learning, as well as the relationship with their Swedish university lecturer(s).

Keywords: International students Sweden, reflections, course structure, learning, cultural and contextual differences

INTRODUCTION

The Swedish government's international higher education strategy for the period 2020-2030 has as its goal to increase Sweden's attractiveness as a knowledge nation, and to be recognized as a leader of quality education and research (Bladh, 2018). Sweden is a country of interest to many international students and can be seen by the increase in international students' numbers studying in Swedish higher education institutions each year. For example, in the academic year 2018/2019 there was a total of 38 330 international students studying in Sweden, these students came from countries such as Germany, France, The Netherlands, China, India, and North America (Swedish Higher Education Authority, (UKÄ), 2020). One reason for the increase may relate to the development of English-taught programs in Swedish higher education institutions, currently there are 1000 English-taught programs on offer across Swedish universities, 100 programs are offered at the postgraduate level and 900 programs are offered at the undergraduate level (see Sweden, (Sverige), 2020).

To date there are few Swedish studies exploring international students teaching and learning experiences in individual courses, rather studies tend to relate to international students' motivations, expectations, and overall cultural experiences studying in Sweden (see Edberg, 2017; Nilsson, 2015; Phang, 2013). Phang (2013) for instance, carried out a qualitative study of eight international teacher education students on their reasons for choosing a Swedish university as their study destination. Three major reasons were identified: 1) a positive first impression from the university website that was associated with relevant and interesting information about courses, programs, and a glimpse into the Swedish lifestyle, 2) the university ranking, and 3) the social activities offered by the university. Nilsson (2015) similarly found that the attractiveness of the university website and course offerings were decisive factors why the 116 international students in his study chose Sweden. Edberg (2017) surveyed 7,196 international students on their experiences of internationalization, and, similar to Phang's and Nilsson's studies, found that the reputation of university and the programs offered via the university website were reasons for student choice studying in Sweden. The findings also noted that most students praised the good teaching staff and their English language skills as well as the excellent library (E-library) resources.

Interestingly one of the goals and focus of the Swedish international higher education strategy is that all Swedish higher education courses support development of intercultural perspectives among all students. The challenge for university teachers is to not only acquire in-depth knowledge of their subject area from an international perspective, but also to develop pedagogical skills to teach students from different teaching and learning backgrounds and traditions (Bladh, 2018). Based on Rodgers' (2002) model of four functions of reflections, the purpose of this qualitative study is to explore the reflections of a small cohort of international student teaching and learning experiences in Swedish university courses. The purpose is to provide key insights, rather than generalisations. Such insights will provide opportunities to make sense of international student learning, enhance and further develop the pedagogical skills and intercultural competencies of the Swedish University teacher.

TEACHING AND LEARNING IN SWEDISH HIGHER EDUCATION

To make sense of international student learning experiences in Swedish courses it is necessary to provide a brief overview (1) how courses are organised and managed in Swedish HE institutions', (2) how the quality of teaching and learning is assured, (3) student teacher relationships, and (4) the purpose of assessment and grading. There are similarities between Swedish course coordination to other universities worldwide for instance, all courses in Swedish HE institutions are organized and managed by course coordinators. Their role involves managing student inquiries, organizing the course content, assessment tasks, and readings. In addition, the role of Swedish course coordinators is to source teaching staff with expertise in both pedagogy and content *in a subject or topic offered in* courses to ensure high quality teaching and learning (Bladh, 2018). This means that individual courses have several teachers from all levels of academia depending on their expertise e.g. lecturers, senior lecturers, associate professors, full professors, and or Directors of programs. The focus on the scholarship of teaching and learning in Swedish HE today is attributed to a report by the Swedish National Union of Students (SFS) (2014) slamming the poor teaching skills among university teachers and demanding immediate improvement. With a focus on the values of HE democracy, internationalisation, gender equality, equal opportunities and sustainability, all university lecturers are required to attend professional development courses to demonstrate abilities to facilitate and engage all students in critical independent thinking, reasoning, reflection and analysis (Bladh, 2018; Karlsson et al. 2016; SFS 2014).

Informal and personal student-teacher relationship and being on first name basis is common in all Swedish universities and can seem strange to some international students used to a more formal relationship such as addressing academic teaching staff by title and surname. Despite the personal teacher - student relationship there is, however, an expectation that all students take individual or personal responsibility for their learning, which involves self-study.

To ensure time for self-study, it is not uncommon for courses to schedule a lecture one day per week and no lectures for the following two weeks, and the duration of lectures may vary between 2 hours to 4 hours depending on the course and the individual academic. Self-study involves students' organizing time for reading, reflecting, and discussing the literature (books, articles, reports etc.) with peers on campus or online. All Swedish Universities provide a great deal of support, for example, academic language support, counselling and/or mentoring to ensure all students succeed in their study that is free of charge. With a focus on student learning and inclusion, students' voices in Sweden are highly valued and student course evaluations are crucial to improving teaching and learning in courses and programs (Karlsson et al. 2016).

In Sweden, it is a common practice to provide both local and international students several opportunities for re-examination or resubmission of work (Swedish Council for Higher Education (UHR), 2020) as well as choice of assessment. There is no national grading system in Sweden, or an overall grade given for a degree (e.g. GPA) as found in other educational systems, which means that students are not ranked. Grades that are provided at the completion of programs or individual courses are, fail (*underkänt*), pass (*godkänt*), pass with distinction (*väl godkänt*), and pass with special distinction (*mycket väl godkänt*). However, this grading system has been recognized as confusing to international students as it is not compatible with that of their home universities grading systems. To address this dilemma and in line with the European Higher Education Area (EHEA) and the Bologna process (European Commission, 2020) most Swedish universities and university colleges have now implemented the European Credit Transfer and Accumulation System or ECTS (European Commission, 2020) following a 6-point grading system: Excellent (A), Very good (B), Good (C), Satisfactory (D), Sufficient (E) and Fail (F).

THEORETICAL FRAMEWORK

The theoretical framework in this study is based on the work of Carol Rodgers (2002) and her model of four functions of reflection. While used to support reflection among teachers (see Corrales., Goldberg., Price., & Turpen, 2020; Eynon & Gambino, 2016), in this study, we will use the model to explore a small cohort of international students' reflections about their learning experiences studying in Sweden. The ways in which these are shown in the different cycles will improve our understanding as teachers and learners to support international students' learning.

Underlying the four functions of reflections are five principles, firstly, reflection on experiences that relate to *personal learning experiences in the classroom*. Secondly, *reflection as both rigorous and systematic*, meaning to slow down the teaching/learning process, to reveal rich and complex details that encourage appreciation, and a way for a considered response rather than a less thoughtful reaction (Rodgers, 2002). The third principle relates to the *formation of a community of respect* where diverse perspectives are both encouraged and welcomed. The fourth principle is *valuing student feedback* that is open, honest, and respectful, and finally the fifth principle, *student learning as guide to teaching* means that in contrast to teaching guiding learning it is learning that guides teaching.

Based on the above principles the four cycles of reflections are: (1) Presence, (2) Description, (3) Analysis and, (4) Experimentation.

(1) *Presence.*
The first phase of the reflective cycle is being present. It is inclusive of *seeing learning, differentiating its parts, giving it meaning, and responding intelligently - in the moment and from moment to moment* that together comprise the process of reflection. Rodgers also explains that presence include qualities of love and passion. Love refers to acceptance of the other as a learner and is free of judgment. Passion means not only a passion for the subject matter but for the human endeavour of learning. Passion also relate to both energy and curiosity that keeps one alert to and engaged with a particular situation or person. For instance, international students often choose to study abroad because of their curiosity for learning, whether it is about (as in this study) the Swedish educational system, politics, gender, or about the cultures of their peers.

(2) *Description*
The process of telling the story of an experience through collaboration. It is in the differentiation and naming of experiences that the diverse elements

explored together and told from many different perspectives makes learning possible. For example, International students' narratives of diverse educational experiences when explored in collaboration provide opportunities for comparative learning, development of cross-cultural understanding and an awareness about themselves as learners.

(3) *Analysis*

Generating several different explanations about what is going on and settling on a theory or hypothesis, that one is willing to test in action. This phase according to Rodgers, is where meaning-making happens.

Understanding the self as a learner is an ongoing process of meaning making. Making sense about choosing to study abroad in a country and university vastly different from that of their own countries (e.g. the Swedish University) provided the international students' opportunities making sense of the differences they experienced while learning about who they were as individuals and learners.

(4) *Experimentation* is about learning to take intelligent action. This cycle follows description and analysis allowing for well thought out and collaboratively constructed theory. For international students, studying in Sweden involves adapting and accepting new ways of learning. For some students it can be challenging, especially when, for example, students' personal learning experiences from their home countries differ to such an extent that new ways of learning in Sweden are perceived as a threat to the self as a learner.

METHOD

The focus of the study was to explore a small cohort of 9 international students' reflections about their learning experiences at a major Swedish university. The students came from countries such as Australia, Japan, Germany, Belgium, the Netherlands, Macedonia, Spain, France, and Canada, enrolled in a variety of education programmes at the university. These students had not previously studied in Sweden and were unfamiliar with the Swedish culture.

The three 30-minute focus group interviews were audio-recorded and transcribed and analysed based on a qualitative content analysis to make sense of the international students' learning experiences studying in the Swedish university (Bengtsson, 2016; Forman & Damschroder, 2008). The use of a small sample size as in this study is not aimed at generalization rather it is about uncovering phenomena in context and situation.

In this study, each individual focus group was assigned a code, for example, Focus Group 1 (FG1), Focus Group 2 (FG2) and Focus Group 3 (FG3), students' individual responses were indicated with the line number found in the interview transcription, for example, FG1 10. The interview data from these focus groups were systematically analysed, and broken down into units, such as, Lectures/Seminars/Tutorials, Teaching/Grading and Student-Teacher relationship and assigned the three primary categories or themes.

(1) Courses. The subcategories that were identified included course content, schedule, and organisation;

(2) Learning and Teaching. The subcategories identified included self-study, assessment, grading;

(3) Relationship with Teachers. The subcategory identified was informal student-teacher relationships.

Thus, the focus of this qualitative analysis was the category system, which was computer-aided with the help of the software for qualitative data analysis MAXQDA in the version Analytics Pro 2018. Working with category systems forms the decisive point of the comparability of the results and thus serves to weigh up the reliability of the qualitative analysis (Forman & Damschroder, 2008). The final part of the analysis was finding explanation and drawing conclusions. Data were checked within the research team through multiple discussions around categorisation and resulted in a form of reflexivity to support the researchers' awareness of their own biases and possible influences.

RESULTS

Courses

All international students' reasons to study at the Swedish university related to its reputation and interest in pedagogy, political studies, comparative education, and particularly, in the areas of special needs and gender education (FG1, FG2, FG3). Some students had chosen courses that aligned to their programs at their home universities and with support from their course coordinator (FG1). Others had relied on the information provided by the university website on the start date and end date of the semester. Course schedules seemed unclear, confusing and "hard to work out" to students who were in Sweden for one semester and needed to be back at the home universities for study commencing second semester (FG1). The problem related to the fact that some courses that began in first semester ran into the beginning of second semester.

Reflecting and comparing the workload at their home universities to that of studying in Sweden most students agreed their workload at home was substantially 'heavier' (FG1, FG3, FG2, 2) as exemplified by a Canadian student:

I have three times like the essays… I have five classes per week and a lot more written exams. We have three written exams per semester per class so that's like 15 exams I have to take like sit down written exams. It's stricter when it comes to essays, referencing, you are not allowed to go in the internet it's only academic journals, peer-reviewed published in the last five years, and the relationship with the teacher too there is no friendship and the classes are a lot bigger…(FG1, 10)

There were also students who experienced the workload similar to that in their home countries: "I find it quite similar to Australia the only difference is my schedule, so in Australia I do like four units whereas here I am only doing two at a time and then once I finished two I'll do two more (FG 2). There was, however, confusion among students about how the lectures were scheduled, "Lectures are not scheduled every week and never in the same room, it´s so confusing. I have to check all the time like it takes time" (FG1, 133). This differed from most students' home countries where courses were offered at the same time each year, classes scheduled weekly, at set times, often in the same rooms, and only the lecturer may change (FG1, 131).

Several of the students were aware before their arrival in Sweden that they would have comparatively less workload than at home (FG2, 2). One student had not imagined the free time to be so extreme: "we have only two afternoons, three hours per afternoon or something like that, so it was even more extreme than I expected", (FG3, 18). While other students were initially confused at the free time, "I think it is more relaxed than I thought - like only having two lectures a week, at first, I was really lost because what did you do with the extra time?" (FG2, 16). Students' concern related to a fear of 'missing out' on studies at home (FG2, 74, 76), though this was not the case for all students: a student from Japan explained:

Before I came here, I was expecting that okay this year is going to be kind of a break for me because like you know, in Japan it was a little bit too stressful, because I had to focus on study. I also need to explore other stuff than study. Getting to know more about various cultures, spend more time thinking about my future or just relaxing, thinking, hanging out with friends, so I am happy that I am here now because finally I have free time for myself as well as time for study (FG3, 27).

Reflecting on the positives of the 'free time' some students noted that "it´s more like here we learn to how to think critically and that´s something I sometimes miss a bit in my (institution)" (FG3, 12). Further, there were students who acknowledged possibilities of concentrating on one or two subjects instead of four, "you have more time for learning it is like a better way for not forgetting it" (FG1, 106). On the other hand, some students identified the free time as problematic, because, compared to their home countries they did not experience learning as much (FG1, 105). A Japanese student reflected on the pros and cons of independent learning:

I am taking two courses…I only go to uni twice a week like, I feel like I have more independence. You have to read and prepare for the class. In Japan, I do pretty much same amount of independent study, reading assignments but I still go to lectures three times a week, for one course. And, well I say they both have pros and cons… personally I wish that I could go to uni more often so that I like keep on studying not only by myself but also with other students, and also I can talk with the professors more often." (FG3, 16).

There was also some discussion about some differences between the Swedish University faculties: "I definitely think it´s our maybe our faculty because I know people who are studying biology and they have lots of work to do and here we are just sitting." (FG2, 57).

Students' initial experiences adapting to learning at the Swedish University caused confusion whether relating to understanding the course schedule, locating classrooms for each topic or making sense of the so called 'free time' or self-study and the accompanying seemingly light workload. There was a concern among some students about a fear of missing out or falling behind in their study at their home universities. However, as students began to settle in there was a growing appreciation and understanding of the 'free time' especially as it related to independent learning encouraging critical thinking and reflection but also time to interact with other students. The students began to see that in Sweden there is an expectation that each student is responsible for their own learning including preparation for classes and relying on the university learning platform (Canvas) for sourcing information e.g. finding the time and location of classes as well as contact information of support personnel including their course-coordinator.

Teaching and Learning

While all students had enjoyed the learning, interaction and discussion offered in the courses (FG1, FG2, FG3). There was also disappointment among some students: "I think the courses that we are taking now have a lot of new opportunities (but) they don´t get it out of that and we are not stimulated that much. […] because you can go very deep in some kind of subjects and that´s not happening "(FG2, 87).

The compulsory readings preceding lectures were also mentioned, and experienced as not taken seriously by some students (FG2, 89) "whereas I found here it is really interesting to read all that stuff but when we were speaking in our groups it sometimes just (did not) go into that deep." (FG2, 38); and "readings are only rarely referred to during the lectures" (FG3, 30). In contrast, reflecting on group discussions in one course, one student felt "we discuss a lot and I feel like this is the most I have learned, the things I have learned is like, to think about my opinion and to hear the opinions of others and this is something we don´t have in Switzerland (FG3, 10). While the students enjoyed sharing perspectives during the small group discussions (FG3, 104), there was a concern about "sharing of opinion" (FG3, 104). One student was particularly critical "I think if it is someone's own opinion then it´s just a personal opinion it´s not how it is in your country well, it can be but it doesn´t need to be"(FG3, 120). There was an agreement among all students about the value of discussions in general "I think it´s important to learn how to speak with other people because you have to respect their opinion you have to wait it´s your turn to talk or that sort of thing" (FG2, 123). Especially discussions relating to the teaching profession "in education it´s very important like because you work with the staff at your school you work with a lot of people when you are a teacher. So I think it´s just they want you to get used to that to work with people because you´re going to do that your whole career" (FG1, 186).

There was an agreement among all students that the examinations tasks differed significantly from their home universities, "a big difference between the Netherlands and Sweden and something I really like is that we are able to choose our own topic for the essay. In the Netherlands, you have one topic and all 30 students are writing about the same thing" (FG3, 29); and "Students experienced less pressure to compete with each other being encouraged to share ideas" (FG3, 135). In particular there was an appreciation for opportunities to resubmit assignments whereas, "In Japan if you don´t submit by the deadline that´s your fault and then you fail and they never give you second chance. Here you can take final exams several times that never happens in my country" (FG3 150). While most students agreed about the positives of the Swedish system there were also students (FG3, 162) reflecting on the positives of the traditional system where competition was a motivating factor to get better grades and exemplified by the following response:

> *"Competition comes with pressure and excitement but it comes with achievement, a bigger feeling of like: wow I am proud of myself you know when you get that 90 and you've worked for it you're like: yes! (FG1 221)*

Reflecting on the pass and fail system several students agreed that the knowledge of passing subjects was relatively easy (FG1, 213, FG2, 140), "and it can be a bit demotivating… like why would I bother studying a lot when you know I can pass and it doesn't matter. At home I am always fighting for the highest grade" (FG2, 140). Another problem with passing or failing subjects related to fairness: "if you put a lot of effort in something and someone else doesn't and you get the same grade, so I am not sure what think about that" (FG2, 137). An alternative perspective related to the importance of feedback as explained by an Australian student:

> *if you're getting the right feedback as well. [...] like if you're just getting pass or fail and then that's it then you don't really know what you're improving on you just know you've passed of failed without any feedback so if you're getting the right feedback then like it's fine in my opinion. (FG1, 214).*

There is no doubt that when relating to examinations or assignments students felt less pressured (FG3, 131 & 150) and they experienced a sense of community with their peers (FG3, 133-135). Nevertheless, the pass and fail system seemed to decrease the motivation and effort among some students knowing that to pass was relatively easy. Nonetheless, what stood out for all students was the support offered at the university and explained by a Japanese student:

> *… The faculty is here to help you if you have problems you can have support, if you have to write something you can also have access to all the libraries - you have always a solution when you have problem… so, I am not stressed at all about my studies. Whereas in my country I am very stressed about everything, like grades, if I am going to have a spot in the library because there are too many people or if I am going to have some help from my teacher because they don't care about you because there are too many students (FG2, 78).*

The main differences and challenges learning in Sweden and agreed by most students related to the focus placed on group work, collaboration and open discussions. For non-English students, reading academic articles in English was particularly stressful. In Sweden there is a requirement for all students to read the required literature attached to each course that include, for example, book chapters, reports, and research articles. To support students to successfully pass the assessment or exams in courses there are hours set aside for self-study or what international students refer to as 'free time' this time is to be used for reading and reflecting about the literature. The student-centred learning experiences, where collaboration, discussions and opportunities for students to openly voice their opinions, made some students feel initially quite uncomfortable. Some students suggested that opinions did not relate to 'deep' scholarly learning. Others enjoyed the opportunity to voice their thoughts and to be able to pose questions. The purpose of the open discussions, collaboration and reflection became clear when students learnt that they were able to choose their own topic to write about for the assessment task.

Choosing their own topic is important as it both motivates the students and it is a way that they feel responsible and part of the learning process (Pereira, Niklasson, & Flores. 2017). All students were surprised to be able to discuss their topics and essays with their peers thus recognizing the benefit of coming together as a community of learners rather than being in competition with each other. The assessment task supported students in confidence building as they were further developing their research skills and especially realizing that the assessment task provided not only deeper and more meaningful learning, but it aligned to the course objectives. Students requiring extra time to submit their essays were surprised at the ease with which they were granted extensions and that there was no penalty or cost involved. The Swedish grading system caused a great deal of discussion among all international students. Some students preferred the traditional system found in their home universities where competition and striving for high grades was both motivating and fun, others were critical of the stress and anxiety that it caused. One student believed that when provided with constructive and fair feedback a grade was not that important; after all it is all about learning, and making mistakes is an integral aspect of the learning journey.

Relationship with Academic Teachers

Most students found the Swedish academic teachers both personable and open to discussions, "I think teachers in Sweden are not afraid to critique, not afraid to like say the real thing and I really appreciate that about the professors" (FG1, 153). Nonetheless, experiencing having several academic teachers teaching in a course was "weird" (FG1, 90), because most students were used to the one academic teacher "the whole semester... here they change" (FG1, 94). The positives of having several academic teachers related to their expertise in the topics they taught, while the negatives related to not being able to form closer relationships, "I think the biggest problem with having a relationship with the teacher here is that you only see him like once or twice. Like you see him for two lessons and then you don´t see him again, whereas in Australia you´re with him for a semester, so you get a closer relationship from the start to the end" (FG1, 155).

To address the academic teachers by their first name was uncomfortable for several students; some students found it disrespectful, and others found it uncomfortable (FG1, 162, FG2, 96, 98, 102). However, students from the Netherlands were used to addressing academic teachers by their first name:
> *I have heard some people they were like: oh I've never done that before and for me that's very normal because we do it all the time and that creates, yes,*

a nice relationship with the teacher and between the teacher and student (FG3, 76).

The consensus among most students was wanting to be taught by academic teaching staff who were enthusiastic, knowledgeable in their topics, approachable, patient and who encouraged and supported students in their learning (SFS, 2014; Karlsson et al. 2016). The fundamental values of higher education in Sweden are democracy, internationalisation, gender equality, equal opportunities, and sustainability. These values underpin and reflect the professional approach to academic teaching and relationships with the students. Swedish academics' informal relationships where students address them by their first name is common in Sweden and clearly confusing to some of the international students. Similarly, unsettling was not having the one and same academic teacher teaching the entire course. This may relate to differences in how learning is perceived in Sweden: that is, learning is the student's personal responsibility, and it is up to the student to initiate contact with academic teaching staff. The casual, friendly and openness of the Swedish academic teachers is reflective of most academic teaching staff. However, there are also Swedish academic teachers who are conservative in nature, who use teacher led approaches where the focus is on teacher talk, rather than student centred learning that encourages discussion, collaboration and relationship building.

DISCUSSION

The lack of small-scale qualitative studies about international student learning experiences in courses in Sweden is often at the cost of quantitative studies that seldom provide the necessary information to support understanding how to support student learning and how to improve teaching skills. In this study Rodgers' (2002) four functions of reflection provided a useful model for understanding international students' learning experiences in different courses at the Swedish University. The model aligns well with the Swedish perspective where reflection on teaching and learning, student-teacher relationships and in particular the centrality of students' voice are central in the improvement of teaching and learning in programs and courses (SFS, 2014; Karlsson et al. 2016). For example, from students' reflections. Feedback suggested improving the university webpages course information such as, clarifying course schedules grades, and self-study.

The four cycles of reflection related to presence, description, analysis and experimentation (Rogers, 2002):

1. Presence- Entry into the cycles of reflection

International students' entry into the cycle of reflection began before their arrival to Sweden. There were several decisions to consider, for examples, their reason and choice of Sweden, the city, the university and the course or courses. Once decisions were made the process of reflection continued together with a curiosity and growing excitement about possibilities for future aspirations, personal growth and sense of self, new learning, ability to adapt to a new country, culture and learning environment as well as making friends.

The evidence of presence related to the international students' curiosity and interest to learn about Sweden, the university culture and about differences between

Swedish teaching and learning to that of their own countries. Students were both committed to learning and willing to adapt to the Swedish University learning culture. While students' reflections suggested initial confusion and stress adapting to the university culture, teaching and learning methods, student-teacher relationship and with several teachers teaching in the course their overall learning experiences after completion of courses were both positive and encouraging.

There was acknowledgment of the Swedish academic teachers' expertise in their topic areas. Their approach was inclusive with a focus on student learning. In particular, their abilities encouraging collaboration, open discussions and group work differed from students' home universities where traditional teaching methods were the norm, for example, teaching and learning is traditional based on teacher talk, information transference from a set text that students are required to learn (Lindblom-Ylänne, Trigwell, Nevgi, & Ashwin, 2006). Secondly, students' experiences of self-study, initially confusing, was received favorably by all students especially after realizing that the so-called free time was meant to be used for reading, reflection, and discussion with peers to allow deep learning.

2&3. Describing and analyzing challenges - Reflecting on the learning experiences

The reorganization and reconstruction of learning experiences through sharing stories was important to students' meaning making and to their sense of self as learners. The small focus groups provided all students opportunities to openly, honestly and critically discuss and share their stories of learning without feeling judged.

International students' challenges adapting to the Swedish university culture was initially described as a confusing time, especially in comparison to their home universities and related to course schedules, teaching and learning approaches, different academic teachers in courses and the free time between lectures. However, while there were students preferring their home universities' organization of courses with set schedules, teacher led lectures with the same academic teacher teaching in all topics, there was recognition of the expertise brought by the different academic teachers in Sweden to their learning. There were also students who believed that missing from their home universities were invitations by the lecturer to engage and provide critical discussions, as indicated by one Australian student comparing lectures at the home university to that of high-school classes.

Discussions about the informal relationships and being on first name with Swedish academic teachers were described as unusual and experienced as uncomfortable by some students. One student, mentioned the difficulty using academics' first names in Sweden and was confused by the friendly and open student-teacher relationship, although this did not relate to all Swedish academics. In contrast to Sweden, the culture at most students' home universities did not encourage students to address academic by their first name, as it was a sign of disrespect.

There were students with a preference for traditional teacher-led methods of teaching and learning to that of the Swedish student-centered approach where discussions, collaboration, and group work is the norm. For example, group work for some of the students meant working towards a common goal, that is, the groups in classes had the same goal, with each group member assigned a particular task to complete. In contrast, group work in Sweden meant students collaborated in choosing a topic of interest and shared the responsibility for organizing their group work without interference from the academic teacher.

4.Experimentation - Self-study and *Learner centered examination*

The initial confusion about the free time between lectures began to make sense to students as they began to adapt to the Swedish learning culture. They learnt that the free time meant time for independent learning or self-study and how they chose to use the time was entirely up to them. Students came to realize the value of self-study in having enough time to read the vast amount of readings (e.g. journal articles, books, reports) they were required to have read to pass the examinations of courses. This was very different from reading one book over 13 weeks as required at their home universities.

The most mentioned and discussed by all the students, related to the learning-centered examination tasks (Pereira, Niklasson, & Flores, 2017) that allowed students to choose a topic based on their personal interest areas and responsibility for their own learning (see Sweden, Sverige, 2020). The examination task supported students' meaning-making and deeper learning in their ongoing intellectual development as learners. To support student learning, both oral and written feedback from examiners are common in Sweden and most courses offer opportunities to resubmit for students who receive a fail grade.

The student-centered learning culture in Swedish higher Education (Lindblom-Ylännea et al., 2006) is about supporting students' ongoing development as learners, encouraging both confidence and self-efficacy (Bandura, 1997; Uusimaki, Garvis & Sharma, 2018). This also means and involves developing trusting relationships, respecting and acknowledging students' capabilities as learners.

IMPLICATIONS

In this study, Rodgers' (2002) reflective study was used as the theoretical framework to provide new meanings to the international student reflections in Sweden. This study provided also new understandings about international student learning experiences in Sweden and thinking about how institutions can further improve in supporting student learning. In particular, the phase of presence is highly important for the set-up of learning approaches. We suggest it is important that transition periods and workshops are possible to support international students with acculturalization into Swedish higher institutions. In particular, a focus is needed on the different organization of courses and the expectations of students around the delivery and tasks implemented within Swedish classes. This also extends to an understanding around different types of examinations and explaining the different relationships with academic teachers. Our small group of participants have given us some insights into particular areas of need for further investigation.

Based on this qualitative study we suggest two key areas for further reflection:

1) Orientation is needed not only about general information within the university, but also on the actual differences in course delivery in Sweden. This could be the introduction of workshops at the start of courses around identified differences.

2) Course leaders of the Swedish international courses must also be aware of cultural differences in learning (Uusimaki, 2018). In particular, they must

ensure academic teaching staff teaching in topics are qualified to provide differentiated support to international students, based on their learning needs.

Finally, we also advocate for increased research on international student learning experiences in Sweden. This study has helped fill a small part of the current void in literature. We suggest that more research is needed on student integration and allowing better transitions within learning approaches, especially under these exceptional times of covid-19.

REFERENCES

Bandura, A. (1997). *Self-efficacy: The exercise of control.* Freeman.

Bladh, A. (2018). *Internationalisation of Swedish higher education and research.* https://www.government.se/information-material/2018/02/internationalisation-of-swedish-higher-education-and-research--a-strategic-agenda/

Bengtsson, M. (2016). How to plan and perform a qualitative study using content analysis. *Nursing Plus Open, 2*(C), 8-14. https://doi.org/10.1016/j.npls.2016.01.001

Corrales, A., Goldberg, F., Price, E., & Turpen, C. (2020). Faculty persistence with research-based instructional strategies: A case study of participation in a faculty online learning community. *International Journal of STEM Education, 7*(21), 1-15. https://doi.org/10.1186/s40594-020-00221-8

Edberg, J. (2017). *Internationella studenter tycker till om sin studietid.* https://www.gu.se/alumn/nyheter-alumn/Nyheter_detalj//internationella-studenter-tycker-till-om-sin-studietid.cid1433944

European Commission. (2020). *The European higher education area Bologna process implementation report 2018.* https://eacea.ec.europa.eu

Eynon, B., & Gambino, L. M. (2016). Professional development for high-impact e-portfolio practice. *Peer Review, 18*(3), 4-8.

Forman, J., & Damschroder, L. (2008). *Qualitative content analysis.* Oxford, U.K.: Elsevier.

Karlsson, S., Fjellström, M., Lindberg-Sand, Å., Scheja, M., Pålsson, L., Alvfors, J., & Gerén, L. (2016). *Högskole-pedagogiskutbildning och pedagogisk meritering som grund för det akademiska lärarskapet.* Sveriges universitets och högskoleförbund (SUFH). https://suhf.se/publikationer/rapporter/

Lindblom-Ylänne, S., Trigwell, K., Nevgi, A., & Ashwin, P. (2006). How approaches to teaching are affected by discipline and teaching context. *Studies in Higher Education, 31*(3), 285-298. https://doi.org/10.1080/03075070600680539

Nilsson, P. (2015). Expectations and experiences of inbound students: Perspectives from Sweden. *Journal of International Students, 5*(2), 161-174. https://doi.org/10.32674/jis.v5i2

Pereira, D., Niklasson, L., & Flores, M. A. (2017) Students' perceptions of assessment: a comparative analysis between Portugal and Sweden, *Higher Education, 73*(1), 153-173. https://doi.org/10.1007/s10734-016-0005-0

Phang, S. L. (2013). *Factors influencing international students' study destination decision abroad.* GUP Göteborgs Universitet, Gothenburg, Sweden.

Rodgers, C. (2002) Seeing student learning: Teacher change and the role of reflection. *Harvard Educational Review, 72*(2), 230–253.

Statistical Central Byrån (SCB). (2019). *Universitet och högskolor Internationell studentmobilitet i högskolan 2018/19.* https://www.scb.se/

Swedish Council for Higher Education, (UHR) (2020). https://www.uhr.se/en/start/

Swedish National Union of Students, (SFS). (2014) *Recommendations on general learning outcomes for the teaching qualifications required for employment as academic teacher and on mutual recognition.* Retrieved from: https://suhf.se/app/uploads/2019/03/REK-2016-1-On-general-learning-outcomes-for-teaching-qualifications_Dnr-024-16.pdf

Swedish Higher Education Authority (UKÄ). (2020). *Higher Education Institutions in Sweden. 2020 Status Report.* https://english.uka.se/about-us/publications/reports--guidelines/reports--guidelines/2020-08-26-higher-education-institutions-in-sweden---2020-status-report.html

Sweden, (Sverige) (2020). *Highly ranked universities.* https://sweden.se/society/higher-education-and-research/

Uusimaki, L. (2018). Teacher Agency. Relational Cultural Theory. In Maurizio Sibilio and Paola Aiello (ed) *Lo sviluppo professionale dei docenti. Ragionare di agentività per una scuola inclusive* (pp.209-305). Edises

Uusimäki, L., Garvis, S., & Sharma, U. (2018). Swedish final year early childhood preservice teachers' attitudes, concerns and intentions towards inclusion. *International Journal of Special Needs Education.* DOI: https://doi.org/10.9782/17-00034

BIOGRAPHIES

Liisa Uusimaki, is an Associate Professor in Pedagogy at the Department of Education and Special Needs Education at the University of Gothenburg, Sweden. Based on her interest and expertise in teaching and learning in higher education she received an Excellent Teacher award in 2018. Her teaching and research areas include; internationalisation, pedagogical and educational leadership, inclusion, identity, mentoring, professional development and developmental psychology. Email: liisa.uusimaki@gu.se

Susanne Garvis is a Professor of Education and the Chair of Department of Education at Swinburne University of Technology. She has extensive experience working within early childhood education around the areas of policy, quality and learning. Her work has also focused on teacher education and the importance of inclusive and democratic ways of working. Email: sgarvis@swin.edu.au

Peer-Reviewed Article
Special Edition | Reflection and Reflective Thinking

© *Journal of International Students*
Volume 10, Issue S2 (2020), pp. 51-70
ISSN: 2162-3104 (Print), 2166-3750 (Online)
ojed.org/jis

A New Country, New University, New School – How Do I Cope? International Student Experiences

Kay Hartwig
Griffith University, Australia

Harry Stokhof
Han University, The Netherlands

Peter Fransen
Han University, The Netherlands

ABSTRACT

Many students embark on an international experience (study tour and/or practicum/placement) during their teacher education program. There are benefits and challenges for those participating in such programs. Reflection is a useful tool in enabling the students to reflect on their experiences; capitalise on the benefits and assist in meeting the challenges that may arise. This paper reports on how reflection was used in a three-week program for international students conducted in a school in The Netherlands. Reflection is an important part of the program as the students are required to socialise into a new country and culture; a new university setting; and then a new school site – multi socialisation (Barton & Hartwig, 2017). The aim of this specific program was the development of participants both as global citizens and as global teachers (Stokhof & Fransen, 2017). Reflection enabled the students to appreciate and understand their experiences in the community of multi international students, foreign pupils and teachers in a foreign school context, thus supporting their development as global citizens and global teachers.

Keywords: study abroad, preservice teachers, global citizens, global teachers

INTRODUCTION

The Australian Government (2020) reported that some 52,000 students travelled overseas for study in 2018. There are both benefits and challenges for students who travel abroad for study. Some of the benefits that have been investigated in the literature have included: personal and professional connections; immersing in a new culture and community; personal growth; new knowledge and expanding horizons. International students may also be faced with challenges as they embrace studying in a new country (Brown, 2009; Hartwig, 2017; Kramer & Wu, 2019; Trede, Bowles & Bridges, 2013). This is compounded when the students are preservice teacher education students and are required to teach in a classroom as part of their study. *Will they understand what I say?* This is a common concern expressed by many international students as they prepare to go into a classroom in a different country with a different native language. Reflection has been used in this program to assist the international students to navigate teaching in a classroom in a new country.

The program under study is a three-week program for international students conducted in a primary and secondary school in The Netherlands. The program has been running for six years and welcomes students from many countries. This paper reports on the experiences of a group of 19 Australian, South African and Indian students involved in the program during January 2020. Reflection is an important part of the program as the students are required to socialise into a new country and culture; a new university setting; and then a new school site – multi socialisation (Barton & Hartwig, 2017). In this specific program, reflection focused on the process of becoming global teachers and global citizens (Stokhof & Fransen, 2017). The aim of the program is for all participants to develop into global teachers or at least be inspired so they will share their experiences when they return to their home country and become global citizens. Reflection enabled the students to appreciate and understand their experiences in the community of multi international students, foreign pupils (the school children) and teachers in a foreign school context, thus supporting their development as global citizens and global teachers. These international experiences and especially the program at HAN University where there is a focus on global citizens and global teachers, helps to prepare pre-service teachers for the future as teachers in the global context but also improves their employability in their home country. The research question for this study therefore was: *What is the effect of multi modal reflection in the program on the participants' awareness of their development as global citizens and global teachers?*

FRAMEWORK AND LITERATURE REVIEW

The Rodgers (2002, p. 230) four functions of reflections are used as the framework in this paper. Rodgers describes a four-phase reflective cycle where she explores the roles of presence in experience: learning to see; description: learning to describe and differentiate; analysis of experience: learning to think critically and create theory; and experimentation in helping teachers slow down and attend to student learning in more rich and nuanced ways. These functions therefore look at reflection as: a meaning-making process, a rigorous way of thinking, being important in and for community and, a set of attitudes. The Rodgers framework allows for a diverse investigation of reflective practices.

Hartwig (2017) used pre and post surveys and students' weekly reflections in her study which ran for three weeks whilst the participants were involved in an international teaching experience. Three main themes were identified: employability, value of the experience and open-mindedness. All the participants (N=53) were pre-service teachers and their focus in the reflections were centred on how the experience would make them a better teacher and assist in making them more employable than their peers who had not taken such an experience. They acknowledged that they were taken out of their 'comfort zone' but believed this enhanced their future teaching career. The pre-service teachers were challenged by being in a country where English is not the home language (in addition some of the Indian and South African teachers have English as their second or third language); teaching in a different school setting; and using the Jenaplan methodology which was new for all participants. The Jenaplan pedagogy was derived through the work of German educator, Peter Petersen in the early 1920's (Azevedo & Ferreira, 2012). Classrooms are not arranged by year levels but in heterogeneous groups. The philosophy promotes children's responsibility and autonomy whereby there is experimentation, collaboration and interaction between children and adults both inside and outside the school. The children are encouraged to talk together, play, work and celebrate differences. The task of the group leader is to let each child work to their own pace.

As well, there can be challenges for both the teaching staff in the university and the teaching staff in the foreign school classroom. These challenges have been identified as teachers dealing with unfamiliar characteristics and diverse needs of international students (Dippold, 2013; Tran & Pham, 2017). Another challenge is the use of pedagogical practices to effectively engage with and use the diversity of cultures, knowledge and experiences to ensure learning for all (Leask, 2009; Tran & Pham, 2017). Berger (2004) describes the teachers in the classrooms as the 'guides' to help student teachers approach their 'knowledge and awareness' (p. 345). The importance is placed on the teachers to support critical cultural reflection to prepare students in their intercultural readiness.

Preparing culturally responsive future teachers has implications for preservice teacher education programs. Providing international study abroad programs through the training of preservice teachers can assist the teachers in becoming mindful of culture and cultural differences. Marx and Moss (2011) found in their case study that explored a teacher completing a semester abroad that the participant became more culturally sensitive, and she was developing 'richer and more complex cultural constructs, exploring her own identity, accepting and recognizing fundamental cultural differences in herself and others, and actively seeking out intercultural experiences as an avenue to continue her intercultural development'. Norman (2020) found that culturally responsive practices can enhance teacher capacity and self-awareness and that all teachers should have a multicultural perspective, so all educators learn the cultural backgrounds of their students and create a classroom environment where students learn from each other. This study provides such culturally responsive practice as both the student teachers and the pupils of the school learn from each other in the classroom

BACKGROUND OF THE STUDY

Participants

Participants (n=19) are pre-service (trainee) teachers from Australia, South Africa and India. All participants attended a three-week program (Teaching in The Netherlands, a Winter Course on Dutch Education) offered at Han University in The Netherlands, during January 2020. All of the pre-service teachers voluntarily decided to take the program. The program included:

> Week 1: Intensive lectures at the university including topics such as Dutch Education System, Dutch Culture and Society, Re-Thinking Education, ICT in Education, Green Schools, and visit to a Steiner School and a Local Public School.

> Week 2: Further intensive lectures at the university on topics that included the Jenaplan Methodology, the Global Teacher, Teaching Global Citizenship, Mind Mapping and a visit to a Jenaplan School and a Montessori School.

> Week 2/3: Teaching in a local primary school using the Jenaplan Methodology or teaching in a secondary school with a mission on Global Citizenship; students were under the supervision of the university staff and the school staff; presentations of their reflections were ongoing throughout the week. Reflections were presented for peers and staff of the university and staff of the schools, using multimodal methods, thus allowing all participants from different countries to explore their own experiences and home country education strategies.

> Additional Activities: There were cultural activities for the preservice teachers, including visits to an Open-Air Museum, the Van Gogh Museum, and a Dutch Highlights Weekend Tour where students were able to sample the cultural and historical aspects of the country.

Engaging students in the reflection process

Reflection, according to Ryan (2013) involves the consideration of associated factors and influences and deciding whether and how to respond or act to improve conditions or outcomes. Multimodal reflections (Barton & Ryan, 2014) enable participants to use various activities that use written, visual, oral or performance modes of expression. A multimodal reflective approach is the basis of the program. The strategies used include:

- Writing a report of 2000 words that describes their ideal school. The report includes the preservice teacher's vision, beliefs and principles on quality education;
- Preparing a visual presentation of their Ideal School, in a Prezi, PowerPoint or Video;

- Giving an oral presentation of the Ideal School to University and School staff and peers;
- Making a reflective poster (see Appendix 1 for an example);
- Sharing the reflective posters to university and school staff and peers;
- Discussions led by the classroom teachers with the individual students focusing on the daily development of teaching practice in the classroom.
- Discussion led by the university teachers in a group setting that focuses on awareness, development in question-driven learning methodology and didactics, new learning points, communication and cultural differences, language barriers, global teacher.

Sample questions posed during these sessions included:
1. What surprised you – for the pupils and yourself?
2. What went well (pupils and yourself)?
3. Did the pupils learn by researching QDL (Question Driven Learning)?
4. How did you solve the language barrier?
5. Which questions from the pupils have now been answered?
6. Did you make new knowledge visible yet for the pupils (for example in your class mind map)?
7. Opinion: "perfection is being open for change". What can you say about this quote regarding yourself?

- Preservice Teachers interview in pairs. Sample questions posed during these sessions included:
  Please share your thoughts and comments on the Teaching Practice at your primary or secondary internship school. Please share your thoughts and comments on the academic content of the Winter course.
- Completing an overall written reflection of the course (at the end of the program).

Chen, Nimmo and Fraser (2009) calls on teachers to critically re-examine their practice to become culturally responsive. They believe this can be done through reflection and have developed a self-study tool to assist beginning teachers on their journey of transforming classroom practice. They believe responsive environments are important and using the tool will lead to a personal and introspective level of reflection that can encourage transformation in culturally responsive teachers. In this study students learn to re-examine current and past practices as a teacher, when operating a novel question-driven learning environment in foreign country. Working with Dutch pupils who are accustomed to exploring learning content by means of self-formulated questions, challenges the students culturally both in a personal as well as in a professional sense. [1]

---

[1] Note: In this paper, the use of the word pupils refers to the children at the school. At times the preservice trainee teachers are referred to as students (meaning student teachers).

METHODOLOGY

This is a mixed methods project using both quantitative and qualitative data. Tashakkori and Teddlie (2003, p. 711) describe mixed methods as "a type of research design in which quantitative and qualitative approaches are used in types of questions, research methods, data collection and analysis procedures and/or inferences. Tashakkori and Creswell (2007) further describe mixed methods as having the investigator collect and analyse data, integrate the findings and draw inferences using both quantitative and qualitative approaches, and/or methods within a single study or program on inquiry. The mixed methods approach used in the study is exploratory which includes quantitative data, qualitative analysis and inference (Tashakkori & Teddlie, 2003). The qualitative data helped to explain and build upon the quantitative results. The data collection included collection of the quantitative data followed by the qualitative data. This design allowed for an interpretation based on both sets of data.

Wise (2014) reported the strengths of mixed methods research. Some of these include:

- Words, pictures and narratives can be used to add meaning to numbers generated as part of data gathered in quantitative processes;
- Numbers can be used to add precision to words, pictures and narratives;
- A research can generate and test with numbers a grounded theory;
- Mixed methods can answer a broader and more complete range of research questions;
- Qualitative and quantitative research when used together can produce a more complete knowledge necessary to inform theory and practice. (p.194)

For the qualitative data, manual coding of themes was undertaken, with clusters being made that informed the variables constructed (Burns, 1998). The quantitative data was entered in the SPSS software program (Connolly, 2007) to calculate the mean and standard deviation. The mixed methods data analysis then involved the integration of the statistical and thematic data.

ANALYSIS

To interpret the qualitative and quantitative data, Rodgers' (2002) four functions of reflections were used as variables in the analysis framework. To align these functions of reflection to the objectives and the content of the educational program under study, the four functions were further operationalized for analysis in sub variables, as explained in the following paragraphs.

Reflection as Meaning-Making Process

Regarding the meaning-making process participants could reflect on two major elements in the program: the experience of the educational content, which was provided by the staff at the University, and the experience of the teaching practice in the workplace. For both elements the data on the variable reflection as a meaning-making process was explored: a) for *interaction* between the students and the environment in the experience, b) for *continuity* between the experience and prior knowledge and previous experiences, c) and for the impact of the experience on students' *development of practical theory*, as suggested by Rodgers (2002).

Reflection as a Rigorous way of Thinking

Rodgers' (2002) construct of "a rigorous way of thinking" was operationalized in this study for the two main objectives of the program. The first objective was the development as a Global Citizen and the second objective was development as a Global Teacher, who teaches global citizenship to others. Table 1 (A) shows how rigorous thinking as a Global Citizen was operationalized in the program as the knowledge and skills which contribute to the reflection process.

Table 1: Operationalization of Knowledge, Skills and Attitudes as Global Citizen and Teacher

(A) Operationalization of Knowledge and Skills as Global Citizens

Sub variables	Contribution to process of reflection on the program	References
Knowledge of various perspectives	"Opens up" the conscious perception that there are different ways to perceive experiences	(Chen, Nimmo, & Fraser, 2009)
Knowledge of cultural differences and similarities	Leads to awareness that personal norms and values might be culturally coloured and not universally valid per se	(Marx & Moss, 2011)
Skill of questioning	Supports the ability to frame and name the problem	(Rodgers, 2002)
Skill of mind mapping	Supports the ability to explore the interrelatedness of ideas by visualizing them in a structure	(Stokhof, De Vries, Bastiaens, & Martens, 2017)
Skill of research	Supports the ability to persistently and carefully test if and to what extent ideas and presumptions held are true on what grounds	(Rodgers, 2002)

(B) Operationalization of Knowledge and Skills as Global Teacher

Sub variables	Contribution to process of reflection on the program	References
Knowledge of the potential of student questioning	"Opens up" the perception to what extent student questions can contribute to teaching and learning	Stokhof et al., 2017)
Knowledge of diversity to meet student needs	Raises awareness about which kind of teacher actions are needed to facilitate student needs in diverse population	(McGrady, 2017)
Skill of using specific didactics	Supports ability to consider how and under which conditions teaching methods have impact on student thinking and learning	(Loughran, 2019)

| The skill of selecting sources and materials | Supports ability to estimate and anticipate on which kind of resources students might need to answer self-raised questions | (Stokhof et al. 2017) |
| Skill of guiding student questioning | Supports ability to estimate and anticipate on which kind of scaffolds students might need to generate, formulate and answer self-raised questions | (Stokhof et al., 2017) |

(C) Operationalization of Attitudes as Global Citizens and as Global Teachers

Variables	Sub variables	Contribution to process of reflection on the program	References
Attitudes as Global Citizen	Open mindedness	Willingness to see and acknowledge new ideas contrary to former held convictions	(Rodgers, 2002)
	Curiosity	Focused interest in learning potential of the experience (cf. Dewey's "Whole-heartedness")	(Rodgers, 2002)
	Inquiry as a stance	Critically examining the real-life implications of the experience	(Cochran-Smith & Lytle, 2009; Rodgers, 2002)
Attitudes as Global Teacher	Allow students' voices	Exploring the potential of supporting self-directed learning	(Stokhof & Fransen, 2017)
	Teacher as coach	Comparing different non authoritative roles as teacher	(Stokhof & Fransen, 2017)
	Release of teacher control	Re-examining the concept of teacher responsibility	(Stokhof & Fransen, 2017)

In contrast to the reflection on the development as Global Citizen, which has a more personal character, is the reflection on the development as Global Teacher more focused on specific professional development. Table 1 (B) shows the sub variables of knowledge and skills which were used to analyse the process of reflection as Global Teacher.

Reflection in Community

Working with a multinational group of preservice teachers opened opportunities for community reflection in the program. Students were invited systematically to communicate their experiences to each other. Formulating their experiences for the group required that they had to get outside the experience and had to seek an appropriate form to connect to the diverse group of listeners. Exchanging experiences was expected to a) open awareness of other new perspectives, b) affirm the value of one's experience, and c) evaluate the nature and value of international collaboration. Major and Santoro (2016) affirm that providing opportunities for reflective conversations during international placement experiences for preservice teachers would further the aim of developing a learning community where all members would learn from each other. Furthermore, Santoro and Major (2012) believe that if the preservice teachers are involved in teaching in a culturally different context, awareness and clarity will be enhanced.

Reflection as a set of Attitudes

As Rodgers (2002) suggested, attitudes can either block or open up the pathway to development during the program. In this study we differentiate between attitudes as Global Citizens and as Global Teachers. Attitudes as Global Citizens refer to the personal attitudes that increase the chance of broadening one's personal field of knowledge and awareness when reflecting on experiences. We consider open mindedness and curiosity to be a prerequisite for international students to become aware of their global citizenship, but also find a positive critical inquisitive stance essential for further development as global citizens. Attitudes as Global Teachers refer to professional attitudes that support open reflection on the impact a teacher has on the development of global citizenship in students (see Table 1 (C). In the program these professional attitudes were aligned to the objective of getting acquainted to more student-centred methods of teaching and awareness of corresponding teacher attitudes (Stokhof & Fransen, 2017).

RESULTS AND DISCUSSION

The purpose and meaning of the Winter Course as an educational program were to contribute to the intellectual, moral and emotional growth of the participants both personally (Global Citizen) and professionally (Global Teacher). The program was designed as a series of experiences to reflect upon, offering encounters with new skills and knowledge which were then applied in the workplace setting. Time was allotted for participants to reflect on the potential significance of the experience and discuss its implications for personal and professional development. We report and discuss in this section how the program supported the international students to reflect on their experiences, using the Rodgers (2002) four functions of reflections as framework for interpretation.

Reflection as Meaning Making Process

Making Meaning of Educational Content

When examining the qualitative data on the *interaction* between oneself and the educational content, we noticed that almost all students actively related this to themselves as teachers: *The educational content provided fresh ideas and examples that could be used within the classroom.* Students perceived that the delivery of the content was interactive and aligned to the objectives of the program: *The lectures where often hands-on and interactive which made the lessons engaging and we were able to see different teaching methods in practice.* Students were even more outspoken about the *continuity* of the experience, when they relate the content to prior knowledge: *The content which was given has great value as it gives a whole new perspective on education as it is done so differently in the Netherlands compared to Australia* and to previous (lacking) experiences: *After participating in the course I realized that the content was linked to something I have only had some exposure to and wanted to see how it translated in the school.*

In many cases we saw examples of how students used the input of the educational content to either build, refine, and/or revise their practical theories. For example, one student describes how she formed new practical theory: *It provided me with an outlook of teaching I had not seen, and I have been able to implement many of the strategies learnt in my daily teaching life.* Another student used the input of the educational content to critically examine (and potentially revise opinions on) the educational system at home: *It was extremely interesting hearing about the differences and similarities in Dutch, South African and Indian education systems. It made me evaluate the Australian system and think about the reasons behind certain choices.*

However, not all students were fully satisfied with the educational content of the program: *There was some educational content that is useful and can be used in my future teaching practice, and some content that has already been covered back home in Australia.* The data supports the hypothesis that students gave meaning to the educational content in such a way that it connected experiences to new levels of understanding and gave an impetus to growth, as suggested by Rodgers (2002, p.850).

Making Meaning of Teaching Practice

When examining the qualitative data on the *interaction* between oneself and the environment of the teaching experience, almost every student felt it was essential to be in the classroom and to experience the question-driven teaching themselves first-hand: *The teaching experience has been extremely valuable in developing my professional skills as a teacher. I believe teaching is a hand-on profession, where the only true way to learn is to attempt the task and experience the students' [pupils] reactions.* The data also shows that students were aware of *continuity* by making explicit connections and relations with prior knowledge and experiences: *The experience allows me to see how education functions in the Netherlands and visually see the difference in the school compared to back home.*

The data showed that the teaching practice had a significant impact on the participants' practical theory. Some students were building new practical theories: *Going out of my comfort zone has been extremely rewarding. Learning new skills and having an idea on how inquiry learning works within the classroom setting has been very insightful.* Other students validated existing practical theories: *The teaching practice demonstrated how providing students with the freedom in deciding their education allows them to become independent and creative individuals.* Sometimes the experiences required more thorough revision of theory: *It was challenging to change everything I thought about teaching, however, I think it was a valuable lesson for me to learn.*

Overall, we conclude that reflection on the teaching experience had a profound impact on meaning making and gave strong impetus for professional development of the participants as teachers. These observations are very similar to findings of Marx and Moss (2012), who reported that immersion in the daily practice of teaching in a foreign school culture can transform preservice teachers' views on education and teaching and set them on a path towards reconsidering formerly held beliefs.

Reflection as Rigorous way of Thinking

In this section we present the quantitative data from the survey for rigorous thinking as Global Citizen and as Global Teacher and illustrate these findings with qualitative data in the form of student citations from the open questions.

Rigorous thinking as Global Citizen

In the survey students were requested to rate the impact of the course. As shown in Table 2 students perceived the course to have substantial to high impact on their development as global citizens (scores 4-5).

Table 2: Impact of Program on Knowledge and Skills as Global Citizen (N=19)

Sub variables	Min.	Max	*M*	*SD*
Knowledge of various perspectives	3	5	4.37	.761
Knowledge of cultural differences and similarities	3	5	4.26	.733
Skill of questioning	3	5	4.58	.607
Skill of mind mapping	3	5	4.58	.607
Skill of research	2	5	4.00	1.155

Scores in the survey show that the impact of the program on knowledge and skills as global citizens has been perceived generally as "substantial" or "high". The experience of the language barrier opened up new perspectives: *Realizing how difficult it is to learn another language and adapt to a whole other environment and culture is not an easy thing to do. This definitely opened my mind on this area for back home.* Almost all students mentioned they became more aware of cultural differences between the nationalities: *I think this experience has enabled me to gain a better understanding and appreciation for the importance of culture, and also its relevance to the teaching profession.* Students also recognized the many differences between the educational systems which became apparent in the reflection sessions: *It was extremely interesting hearing about the differences and similarities in Dutch, South African and Indian education systems.* Regarding the development of skills as global citizens, students considered the impact of the program also to be high, especially for questioning and mind mapping: *I will definitely be teaching my students the mind mapping skills that Harry taught us to develop effective questions. Mind mapping is probably the biggest thing I will take from this course. It is such a simple task that can be applied to everything.* However, the impact of the program on development of research skills was considered to be relatively lower: *I believe the Winter Course could have developed researching more, as I do not think we spent a lot of time on developing our skills as teachers to do this.*

If we analyze the data from the perspective of four stages in the reflection process, as suggested by Rogers (p. 856), many students seem to surpass the stages of perplexity and mere description of the experience and were able to analyze the impact it had on their knowledge and skills as global citizens. Some students reflect on the character of their personal learning process: *Being forced to work with people from different countries with different viewpoints has been a very steep learning curve, although it has been difficult sometimes to step out of my comfort zone I think it has been a valuable experience for my growth.* Others were able to describe a fundamental change in their views: *I think the biggest realization/change of perspective I had during this experience was the fact that the Dutch and the Indians made allowances for the Australians by speaking English. My view was switched from 'they don't speak English as well as us' to 'wow, they are speaking English to allow for us to be able to communicate with them.*

Rigorous Thinking as Global Teacher

As shown in Table 3, students perceived the course also to have substantial to high impact (scores 4-5) on their development of knowledge and skills as a global teacher, especially on the guidance of student questioning and the potential it has for teaching and learning.

Table 3: Impact of Program on Knowledge and Skills as Global Teacher (N=19)

Sub variables	Min.	Max	M	SD
Knowledge of the potential of student questioning	3	5	4.53	.612
Knowledge of diversity to meet student needs	1	5	4.11	1.100
Skill of using specific didactics	2	5	4.05	.848
Skill of selecting sources and materials	3	5	4.16	.898
Skill of guiding student questioning	2	5	4.42	.838

Students reflected on their development of knowledge and skills as global teachers. Many of them recognized the potential of student questioning: *This experience has demonstrated the potential that student questioning has in terms of their learning. I noticed that when students are able to determine their own learning, it generates their interest and consequently they become motivated to participate in their learning.* The experience of teaching students from a different culture and in another language made a deep impression on most participants: *Acknowledging diversity in the classroom has always been important to me. Now that I have some experience in teaching students from a different culture and language it is even higher for me.* However, one student did not feel the course had any impact on her knowledge of diversity: *I have always had the ability to acknowledge diversity in the classroom, so I don't believe this course impacted in that sense. It is your responsibility as a teacher to naturally acknowledge diversity.* Several students considered learning and using specific didactics useful: *I was able to experience and implement different teaching techniques.* But some were critical on the limited offer of specific didactics: *I believe we have only had a few skills shown to us, and we would have benefited in being shown the use of different didactics.* Students recognized the importance of the skill for selecting sources and materials for student inquiry: *It also highlighted the importance of providing sources and materials for student inquiry to ensure they are heading in the right direction without providing them the answers and allowing them to discover it for themselves.* Many students reflected positively on the development of their skills to guide student questioning: *I was able to let the children research and find their own knowledge and understanding only guiding them when needed.*

Looking at the data from the perspective of the stages of reflection, almost all students were able to analyze the impact of the experience on their professional development and to consider future experimentation. Several students described growing feelings of competence: *The skills I learnt from the questioning seminar will be very beneficial when I teach in a classroom. I was not very confident in this area but now I believe I will be able to implement this well.* Other students formulated new questions that rose out of the experience, naming their need for more in-depth development: *I think question driven learning is great however I am still not sure how to TEACH students to come up with effective questions. The students came up with great questions however I did not teach them that skill, they already had the skill.* Some considered future applications of the experience: *The content I valued as I can take what I have learnt and apply pieces into my classroom back into Australia.* Yet others were triggered to dig deeper and search for the rationale of the educational system in their home country: *It made me evaluate the Australian system and think about the reasons behind certain choices.* Some even contemplated about the real-life challenges when willing to apply the new-found knowledge and skills at home: *I think the difficult task will be finding a balance between students choosing what they want to learn and ticking off content descriptors from the Australian Curriculum.*

If we contrast these findings with Bennett's (2004) Developmental Model of Intercultural Sensitivity (DMIS) we see that most students are in the ethnorelative stages of "acceptance", "adaptation" and sometimes even "integration" (pp. 62-63). The results show that students open themselves up to new cultural teaching experiences, seek meaning in them for themselves and explore if and how their experiences can be integrated in their own future practice.

Reflection in Community

The international students were systematically invited to collectively reflect on their experiences during the program. Sharing their experiences, ideas and questions in the community broadened and deepened their reflections. Four effects of the collective reflection are mentioned by the participants. First, it opened awareness of other new perspectives: *I think I gained most of my knowledge on global perspectives from the discussions we had with people from different cultures during seminars.* Second, by sharing reflections the value of one's experience was affirmed: *Every time something happened that I would consider unusual my teaching partner from Australia, and I would say how that would never happen back home, but why not? I think we can get stuck in our own ways of doing things and our expectations of our students. This experience has helped me see students in a different light.* Collective reflection also contributed to the evaluation of the nature and value of international collaboration. Some students expressed their growing appreciation of efforts to bridge the language barrier: *Working with the Indians I learnt to appreciate the fact that my first language is English and must appreciate that they are speaking another language which requires a lot.* Although the language barrier was overcome in all cases, one student still struggled with differences in work-ethics between cultures: *My main concern about co-teaching was the work ethic from my partner compared to myself. I felt I was the only one putting in the time and effort required.* Finally, collective reflection led to a growing awareness not only of differences in the community but also of shared objectives and concerns: *I was surprised at how very different all our cultures and communities are, but also how similar the challenges we face as teachers and beginning teachers are.*

The findings show that heterogeneity in the community of students made them aware that they had different cultural identities which had formed their ideas and behaviour (Chen, Nimmo, & Fraser, 2009). Their communication revealed the cultural gap among them, because previously formed cultural values and practices of the students directed their interpretations of the experiences (Marx & Moss, 2011).

Reflection as set of Attitudes

The impact of the program on their attitudes was scored by the students for both the personal dimension as Global Citizens, as well as the professional dimension as Global Teachers in the survey, see Table 4.

Table 4: Impact of Program on Attitudes as Global Citizen and Global Teacher (N=19)

Variables	Sub variables	Min.	Max	M	SD
Attitudes as	Open mindedness	1	5	4.26	1.147
Global Citizen	Curiosity	3	5	4.68	.582
	Inquiry as a stance	3	5	4.58	.607
Attitudes as	Allow students' voices	1	5	4.47	1.020
Global Teacher	Teacher as coach	3	5	4.58	.607
	Release of teacher control	4	5	4.68	.478

Scores for the impact of the program on the attitudes were generally substantial to high, with two remarkable exceptions (in both cases only one student giving the 1 score). Most students were surprised by how their minds had been opened and they had learnt new ways of teaching: *I did not expect this course would open my mind in such a way as it did. From learning about different cultures, reflecting on my own teaching pedagogies and being able to experience different ways of teaching and learning were just some experiences that opened my mind.* However, one student argued that the program had little impact on her open mindedness: *As being already open minded in the course, I don't believe that the course has given me a further high impact in developing as a global citizen. I have had such a high curiosity in learning about global citizenship as this is a topic that I will need to know of when teaching my students in the future.* Many students mentioned that the program had made them curious: *If we want to learn new things then it is very necessary to open the windows of our mind. This course is helpful for me. I became curious when I saw the students' activities and surroundings of the school.* The program triggered many student's inquisitive stance: *During lessons I was highly engaged and curious to learn as much information about new ways of teaching as possible.* The place of the student's voice in the question-driven curriculum startled almost all students: *Watching as the teachers step back and allow students to have control over their learning has been an eye-opening experience".* Participants revised previous held ideas because of this experience: *I gained a lot from the students in my class, they taught me about the importance of working independently, expressing your beliefs and discussing issues which might typically be avoided in Australia.* The students also reflected on the new 'teacher as coach' role, which contrasted earlier experiences: *I felt as though the relationship that teachers in The Netherlands had with their students was considerably more valued, than from what I had experienced in Australian classrooms.* Finally, teacher control is often the focus for preservice teachers when they undertake placements in the school setting. They are often assessed on how well they control the classroom and the pupils. Many realized that stepping back and allowing the students responsibility was at first difficult, but they learnt that this strategy was worthwhile: *Students need to understand that they are heard and by giving responsibility to the students you develop their self-regulatory skills. This program let me release teacher control and give the students more responsibility.*

Reassessing one's position as a teacher is often hard, especially for new starting teachers just learning the profession. The exposure to a new challenging form of teaching and the supportive collective reflection on these experiences seemed to trigger the inquisitive stance which according to Cochran-Smith and Lytle (2001) is a fundamental prerequisite for their development as teachers.

CONCLUSION

The success of this three-week program offered at HAN University for preservice teachers can be attributed to the dedication of the staff at both the university and the local school. The use of reflection by all involved in the program gave helpful insights which meant improvements could be made as the program progressed. The positive environment both at the university and the school allowed the international students to feel supported and able to reflect deeply on their experiences and where improvements could be made. Therefore, the students were prepared for global experiences they may face in the future as teachers in global contexts. They demonstrated an openness, strategies and experience to cope with diverse situations they may encounter. Their lives have been changed forever as they consider themselves global citizens who "have an open mind, with respect for all and knowledge of all cultures and world issues" (Hartwig, 2017, p. 236). Stokhof and Fransen (2017) acknowledge that teachers play an important role in global citizenship education, being both a source of knowledge and a role model for global citizenship. Hunter, Pearson and Gutierrez (2015, p.1) believe that enabling opportunities for preservice teachers to have such experiences will help to ensure that the next generation of teachers will "understand others first and themselves second" (Barton et al., 2017).

An important question to ask is whether this program is achieving these aims? To conclude, comments are presented from students who completed the program and are now graduated and teaching in schools.

When I first decided to do the winter course, I did not value global citizenship but from participating in the winter course it has opened my eyes and helped me in my current educational practice. It aids me in connecting with students that have different backgrounds. (Graduated participant.)

The winter course enabled me to see curiosity, open mindedness, and inquiry driving student learning and teacher attitude. This is not something that I would had gotten to experience within an Australian classroom and has had a significant impact on my teaching as I aspire to provide these engaging and meaningful learning experiences within my own classroom. (Graduated participant.)

The above comments are testament to the long-term benefits of short-term study abroad programs for students. Ruth, Brewis, Blasco and Wutich (2018) reported that based on qualitative and quantitative analysis of post-graduation data by 118 participants who took part in short-term study abroad programs, positive self-reported impacts across a range of domains relevant to longer academic and career success were identified. The challenge for higher education institutions is to enable all preservice teachers the opportunity to engage in an international experience during their training. As well, the inclusion of reflective activities encourages future teachers to adopt and implement strategies that allow the student voice to be present in the classroom and for global citizenship and global teachers to become part of a natural progression in teacher education. Reflection is now a crucial element in all teacher education programs, assisting teachers in becoming more reflective (Calderhead & Gates, 2003); stimulating teachers' awareness of the causes and consequences of their actions (Carr & Kemmis, 1986), and thus aiming to enable future teachers to be a critical part of shaping future directions in education.

REFERENCES

Australian Government. (2020). *Australian students overseas.* https://internationaleducation.gov.au/research/australianstudentsoverseas/pages/australians-students-overseas.aspx

Azevedo, S., & Ferreira, F. I. (2013). Participation and learning in a Jenaplan School in the Netherlands: An ethnographic research with children. *Procedia-Social and Behavioral Sciences, 82*, 599-603.

Barton, G. M. & Ryan, M. (2014). Multimodal approaches to reflective teaching and assessment in higher education: A cross disciplinary approach in creative industries. *Higher Education Research and Development, 33*(3), 409-424.

Barton, G. M. & Hartwig, K. (2017). *Professional learning in the work place for international students: Exploring theory and practice.* Cham, Switzerland: Springer.

Barton, G. M., Hartwig, K., Bennett, D., Cain, M., Campbell, M., Ferns, S., Jones, L., Joseph, D., Kavanagh, M., Kelly, A., Larkin, I., O'Connor, E., Podorova, A., Tangen, D., & Westerveld, M. (2017). Work placement for international students: A model of effective practice. In G. M. Barton & K. Hartwig (Eds.), *Professional learning in the workplace for international students: Exploring theory and practice,* (pp. 13-34). Springer.

Bennett, M. J. (2004). Becoming interculturally competent. In J. Wurzel (Ed.), *Toward multiculturalism: A reader in multicultural education* (pp. 62-77). Intercultural Resource Corporation

Berger, J. (2004). Dancing on the threshold of meaning: Recognizing and understanding the growing edge. *Journal of Transformative Education, 2*(4), 336-351.

Brown, L. (2009). The transformative power of the international sojourn: An ethnographic study of the international student experience. *Annals of Tourism Research, 36*(3), 502-521.

Burns, R. (1998). *Introduction to research methods.* Longman.

Calderhead, J., & Gates, P. (Eds.). (2003). *Conceptualising reflection in teacher development.* Routledge.

Carr, W., & Kemmis, S. (1986). *Becoming critical.* Falmer.

Chen, D. W., Nimmo, J., & Fraser, H. (2009). Becoming a culturally responsive early childhood educator. *Multicultural Perspectives, 11*(2), 101-106.

Cochran-Smith, M., & Lytle, S. L. (2001). Beyond certainty: Taking an inquiry stance. In A. Lieberman & L. Miller (Eds.), *Teachers caught in the action: Professional development that matters*, (pp. 45-58). Teachers College Press.

Connolly, P. (2007). *Quantitative data analysis in education: A critical introduction using SPSS.* Routledge.

Dippold, D. (2013). Interaction for learning in the Anglophone university classrooms: Mastering interactional challenges through reflective practice. *Journal of Academic Language and Learning, 7*(1), A14-25.

Hartwig, K. (2017). The study abroad programme: Experience and benefits. In G. M. Barton & K. A. Hartwig (Eds.), *Professional Learning in the Work Place for International Students,* (pp. 225-238). Springer.

Hunter, C.A., Pearson, D. & Gutierrez, A.R. (2015). *Interculturalization and teacher education: Theory to practice.* Routledge.

Kramer, D. & Wu, J. (2019). A hope for study abroad: Evidence from Tennessee on the impact of merit-aid policy adoption on study abroad participation. *Educational Policy,* 1-30. https://doi.org/10.1177/0895904818823752

Leask, B. (2009). Using formal and informal curricula to improve interactions between home and international students. *Journal of Studies in International Education, 13*(2), 205-221.

Loughran, J. (2019). Pedagogical reasoning: the foundation of the professional knowledge of teaching. *Teachers and Teaching, 25*(5), 523-535.

Major, J. & Santoro, N. (2016). Supervising an international teaching practicum: building partnerships contexts. *Oxford Review of Education, 42*(4), 460-474. https://doi.ork/10.1080/03054985.2016.1195734

Marx, H., & Moss, D. M. (2011). Please mind the culture gap: Intercultural development during a teacher education study abroad program. *Journal of Teacher Education, 62*(1), 35-47.

McGrady, K. (2017). *Educating for diversity: How to ensure teacher success in reaching culturally and linguistically diverse populations.* Unpublished doctoral dissertation, Johns Hopkins University.

Norman, T, (2020). *Creating inclusive classrooms through culturally responsive pedagogy.* Theses and Dissertations. Norman University. https://rdw.rowan.edu/etd/2759

Rodgers, C. (2002). Seeing student learning: Teacher change and the role of reflection. *Harvard Educational Review, 72*(2), 230-253.

Ruth, A., Brewis, A., Blasco, D., & Wutich, A. (2018). Long-term benefits of short-term research-integrated study abroad. *Journal of Studies in International Education, 23*(2), 265-280. https://doi.org/10.1177/1028315318786448

Ryan, M. (2013). The pedagogical balancing act: Teaching reflection in higher education. *Teaching in Higher Education, 18*(2), 144-155.

Santoro, N. & Major, J. (2012). Learning to be a culturally responsive teacher through international study trips: transformation or tourism? *Teaching Education, 23*(3), 309-322. http://dx.doi.org/10.1080/10476210.2012.685068

Stokhof, H. J. M., De Vries, B., Bastiaens, T., & Martens, R. (2017). How to guide effective student questioning? A review of teacher guidance in primary education. *Review of Education, 5*(2), 123-165. doi:10.1002/rev3.3089

Stokhof, H., & Fransen, P. (2017). "Let's focus on exploration": Developing professional identity of international students as global teachers in a question-driven practicum. In G. M. Barton & K. A. Hartwig (Eds.), *Professional learning in the workplace for international students: Exploring theory and practice* (pp. 239-258). Springer.

Tashakkori, A., & Creswell, J. (2007). Exploring the nature of research question in mixed method research. *Journal of Mixed Methods Research, 1*(3), 207-212.

Tashakkori, A. & Teddlie, C. (2003). *Handbook of mixed methods in social and behavioral research.* Sage.

Tran, L. T., & Pham, L. (2017). International student connectedness with local teachers and peers: Insights from teachers. In Tran, L.T. & Gomes, G. (Eds). *International Student Connectedness and Identity – Transnational Perspectives.* Springer.

Trede, F., Bowles, W. & Bridges, D. (2013). Developing intercultural competence and global citizenship through international experiences: academics' perceptions. *Intercultural Education, 24*(5), 442-455.

Wise, S. (2014). Mixed methods: The third research community. In K. Hartwig (Ed.), *Research methodologies in music education,* (pp. 183-198). Cambridge Scholars Publishing.

Appendix 1: Sample of a student reflective poster

BIOGRAPHIES

Kay Hartwig is a Senior Lecturer, Griffith University, Brisbane, Australia. Dr Hartwig, as well as teaching in the discipline of music (undergraduate to PhD level students), is the Director of internationalisation for the School of Education and Professional Studies. In this role she coordinates study tours for Australian Student Teachers internationally. As well as music and arts education research, her research interests are currently centred around international education; internationalisation of the curriculum; work placements for international students. She is the co-author of the book *Professional Learning in the Workplace for International Students* with Associate Professor Georgina Barton. Kay is the international secretary of ANZARME (Australian and New Zealand Association for Research in Music Education). Email: k.hartwig@griffith.edu.au

Harry Stokhof is a Senior Lecturer at HAN University of Applied Sciences, Nijmegen, The Netherlands. In addition to teaching Bachelor and Master students in Educational Sciences, Harry is involved as a researcher in various design-based projects intended to professionalize teachers in designing and guiding Question-Driven Learning. In close collaboration with various practitioners, colleague teacher educators and scholars, Harry developed a "principle-based scenario for guiding effective student questioning". This scenario is also used for in the yearly Winter Course for international students to introduce Question-Driven Learning in their workplace. Together with Peter Fransen, Harry contributed a chapter to the book *Professional Learning in the Workplace for International Students*. Harry is member of the Board of Directors of EAPRIL (European Association for Practitioner Research on Improving Learning). Email: harry.stokhof@han.nl

Peter Fransen is a Senior Lecturer, HAN University of Applied Sciences, Nijmegen, The Netherlands. Peter teaches Geography, History and Social Sciences at the College of Education for Primary School Teachers of HAN University of Applied Sciences in The Netherlands. Peter is an expert in the pedagogy of Interactive Teaching and Global Citizenship Education. He is a great advocate for internationalization abroad and at home and organizes for example yearly visits for students to the European Parliament's teaching programs. As well as teaching the Dutch students, Peter is actively involved in various teaching programs for visiting international students. Together with Harry Stokhof, Peter contributed a chapter to the book *Professional Learning in the Workplace for International Students*. Email: Peter.Fransen@han.nl

Peer-Reviewed Article
Special Edition | Reflection and Reflective Thinking

© *Journal of International Students*
Volume 10, Issue S2 (2020), pp. 71-85
ISSN: 2162-3104 (Print), 2166-3750 (Online)
ojed.org/jis

Reflecting on Diversity through a Simulated Practicum Classroom: A Case of International Students

Mark Finn
Sivanes Phillipson
Wendy Goff
Swinburne University of Technology, Australia

ABSTRACT

This study aimed to investigate how international students draw on their own cultural identity to reflect on their teaching practice in a simulated classroom in the Australian context. Each simulated teaching session that the students participated in was recorded and sent to the pre-service teachers for later review and reflection. The pre-service teachers were required to produce a 1000 word written reflection of their teaching practice with an explicit focus on how they supported culture, difference and diversity of need in their lesson. Using the Rodger's framework, these reflections were analyzed using the Leximancer software, a lexical semantic tool, to identify the shared and unique experiences that pre-service teachers from the diverse backgrounds face in refining and developing their teaching practice. By highlighting such similarity and difference, it is anticipated that higher education institutions will be in an informed position with regard to the impact of cultural background to teaching practice especially in relation to international pre-service teachers.

Keywords: culture, diversity, pre-service teachers, reflect, simulated practicum.

Changes to migration patterns combined with continued growth in the market for international education mean that the Australian classroom environment of today is more diverse than ever before, both in terms of students and their teachers. This means that a recognition of cultural diversity and the challenges and opportunities it presents must be part of pre-service teacher training. This paper focuses on an innovative approach to supporting diversity and inclusivity in teacher education, using computer-simulated classroom environments and reflective practice. The study aimed to investigate the extent of how pre-service teachers' diverse backgrounds affect their reflections of their interactions within this simulated context, using Rodgers' principles as the analytic framework.

This paper begins with a comprehensive review of the literature on approaches to diversity especially in light of current educational practices. This review is meant to reveal not only existing practices in school teaching but also the advantages and challenges that the diversity of international students brings to current classroom pedagogy.

APPROACHES TO DIVERSITY

The topic of cultural diversity in the classroom has, not surprisingly, been the subject of tremendous academic interest, with scholars identifying a range of both opportunities and challenges (Hattie, 2009). A scrutiny of recent literature on the topic reveals several key themes that frequently appear.

The first of these themes relates to the effect that diversity has on education. Even though most researchers agree that increased levels of diversity among students and staff has a positive effect on the experience of education, there are differing views on how that effect presents. For example, a 2001 study of American high schools found that increased levels of diversity produced an identifiable increase in academic performance (Terenzini et al., 2001). This finding was supported by a 2010 PISA-based study, which identified a clear educational advantage to having a diverse student cohort, as reflected in standardized test results (Konan et al., 2010). More recently, a 2019 German study found that academic performance improved with increased levels of diversity, although in this case the improvement was also tied to psychosocial factors such as feelings of belonging to the school community (Schachner et al., 2019).

Though much of the literature focused on the benefits of cultural diversity in the classroom, there are many researchers who focused on the challenges associated with implementing diversity-orientated strategies. As Harris and Alexander (1998) noted:

> Policy and reform initiatives, such as detracking and inclusion, have also increased classroom diversity. Students who face significant challenges and difficulties in the classroom—due to social inequities or inequalities, language challenges, disabilities or other factors— may in fact require more extensive, scaffolded, and explicit instruction to develop skills, processes, and understandings that other students learn more easily. (p. 122)

Language competence is seen to be one of the most challenging elements of a culturally diverse classroom. For example, Hammond (2001) found that Australian students from non-English speaking backgrounds consistently underperformed on assessment that was designed for native English speakers, a finding that was also found by Cheng et. al. (2007) in Canadian classrooms. These challenges are often exacerbated by the anxiety many students experience when working with unfamiliar language, which leads to what Lou and Noels (2020) have termed a vicious cycle. Indeed Cousik (2015), found that issues around language competency tended to compound other issues that students might face, such as learning disabilities. From a policy perspective, many schools struggle with the tension between assessing students in a dominant language while simultaneously recognizing the importance of their native language abilities (Janmaat, 2012). Importantly, language competency has also been recognized as a challenge for pre-service teachers, especially in the context of a practicum experience (Gan, 2013).

Several studies have sought to explore how the attitudes of teachers relate to broader community beliefs about ethnicity and multiculturalism. Horenczyk and Tatar (2002), for example, have looked at how the attitudes of Israeli teachers have been impacted by broader debates around refugees in the region. Similarly, Forrest et al., (2016) investigated the attitudes of teachers toward cultural diversity in Sydney, Australia. The authors found that there was a complex interaction between teacher attitudes and the beliefs of the wider community in which they worked. Studies such as these make an important contribution to understanding the dynamics of teaching in a culturally diverse environment in that they firmly situate the practice of teaching within its broader societal context.

Given the importance of attitudes to teaching effectively in a culturally diverse context, it is not surprising that a significant amount of the literature in this area is focused around pre-service teacher education. Many teacher education courses now feature elements specifically designed to increase students' capacity to manage diversity in the classroom. Whilst most agree with the value of these initiatives, some have questioned their ongoing impact (Weisman & Garza, 2002). Bryan and Atwater (2002) noted that many teachers graduate from teacher education programs with a worldview that remains situated in their own social and cultural backgrounds. These authors argued that experience of a diverse classroom environment should form a key component of all teacher training program, with others such as Chou (2007) suggesting models such as professional developments schools might offer a possible solution. However, Gay (2010) took this debate a step further to argue that even when pre-service teachers are explicitly introduced to issues of diversity in the classroom there is often some measure of resistance, based on pre-existing beliefs around culture and race. The kind of reflective practice explored in this paper has the potential to alleviate many of these concerns.

Finally, and most importantly in terms of the focus of this paper, there is a body of literature that explores how the cultural background of the teachers themselves affect their teaching strategies. Wulandari (2019), for example, argues that "teachers cannot be separated from their cultural background" (p.49), noting that a teacher's cultural background is likely to affect the way they think, their classroom behaviour, their value systems and their attitudes toward traditions and beliefs. Previously, Dickar (2008) found that American teachers from ethnic minorities had a better understanding of the issues facing students from diverse cultural backgrounds. This finding is even more pertinent when compared to practices of other teachers who predominantly engaged in a variety of strategies that worked to de-emphasize issues of diversity. This finding is supported by similar research in New Zealand, which found that having an ethnically diverse teaching staff benefitted all students, not just those from minority backgrounds. Of particular importance here was the role of teachers from ethnically diverse backgrounds in preparing students for an increasingly multicultural workforce and society (Howard, 2010, p.6).

In a similar vein, there has been research on how diversity impacts on the implementation of educational curriculum. Khine and Fisher (2004) argued that a teacher's cultural background does not just affect the way they handle diversity in the classroom, but actually impacts the way the curriculum is presented. Drawing on earlier cross-cultural comparisons, the authors argued that there are distinct differences in the pedagogical approaches taken by teachers from Western and Asian backgrounds, and these differences were clearly perceived by the students in their classes. These differences were apparent in a number of different dimensions including the extent to which the teacher was willing to help students with their work, the extent to which classroom activities were task orientated and the extent to which all students were treated equally (Khine & Fisher, 2001). More recently, Phillipson and Phillipson (2020) in their study of 37 expert teachers from Australia, Finland, Hong Kong and the United States noted that the cultural background of the teachers determined the way they approached and established relationships with their students from diverse backgrounds, though individual cultures had their own idiosyncrasies that made their classroom practice nuanced.

Lindsey (2004) stressed that although research pointed to a clear connection between a teacher's cultural identity and their classroom practice, this connection was not necessarily reflected on and recognized by the teachers themselves. This disjunction is where reflective practice can be beneficial as "its resonance with teaching is attributable to the fact that it encapsulates the complex, analytical and inquiring nature of teaching" (Harford & MacRuairc, 2008, p. 1885). Loughran (2010) pointed out that expert teachers are reflective and therefore are able to take risks as they learn to manoeuvre their classroom practice. In other words, reflective practice allows teachers to explore how their cultural identity and background influences their teaching practice. This idea of reflexivity, especially within an initial teacher education setting, represents the main focus of the present study. The next section explores literature on how pre-service teachers are prepared for classroom practice and a pathway to reflective practice, including the implications of this preparation for international students. International students in this study are defined as students who were born in a country other than Australia, who have completed their own schooling in their home country but who have chosen to undertake all of their tertiary education in Australia. In this study we define cultural diversity as perceived divergences from white monolingual backgrounds (Dee & Henken, 2002); cultural identity as a conscious identification and perceived membership within a specific group (Collier & Thomas, 1989); and teacher identity as a conscious identification and perceived membership within the teaching profession.

PRE-SERVICE TEACHER PREPARATION

The dichotomy of theory and practice has posed a significant challenge to higher education institutions since Initial Teacher Education (ITE) moved into the university context (Loughran & Hamilton, 2016). Traditionally, universities have been espoused as the contexts that develop theoretical knowledge, and schools have been espoused as the contexts in which initial teacher education students (pre-service teachers) gain their practical understandings. A continuous criticism of ITE lies in the theory-practice nexus and the need for higher education institutions to *bridge-the-gap* (Allen, 2008; Darling-Hammond, 2016). According to Loughran and Hamilton (2016), the consequence of perceiving theory and practice as a dichotomy in the preparation of classroom teachers narrows thinking and leads to a view that only time in schools can develop practical understandings. This view has implications for pre-service teachers who have limited time for reflection and must shift between their student and teacher identity as they travel in and out of their two contexts. Moving beyond the dichotomy of theory and practice opens new ways of reconceptualising ITE and embracing new ways of teacher preparation.

The potential of Virtual Reality (VR) and simulated learning environments is now being realized, adopted and researched across different discipline areas of the higher education context. VR simulations have been successfully utilized in disciplines such as nursing, engineering and medicine to nurture reflection and reflective practice as well as to support the development of professional identity (Elliman, Loizides & Loizou, 2016). Despite this uptake, examining the effectiveness of VR simulated learning environments in ITE appears to remain elusive. This gap is reflected in the limited published research in ITE (McGarr, 2020), and in the traditional theory-practicum models still found in most ITE programs. In fact, in a systematic review of the use of VR simulations in ITE programs Billingsley and colleagues found a mere seven studies that reported evidence on the effectiveness of VR simulations in initial teacher preparation (Billingsley, Smith, Smith & Meritt, 2019).

Despite the limited research in the field, there is some emerging literature that has demonstrated the potential of VR simulation for teacher preparation. For example, in a study that explored the use of mixed-reality simulations prior to and within the practicum experience, Piro and O'Callaghan (2019) reported the VR simulated experience as a major contributor to shaping and developing teacher identity. A VR simulation was employed in the study to expose pre-service teachers to three levels of concepts considered critical and specific to the discipline – threshold concepts. The threshold concepts were (1) rapport building, (2) implementing organizational routines, (3) implementing norms and routines for classroom discourse and work, (4) eliciting and interpreting individual students' thinking using a graphic organizer, and (5) leading a group discussion with higher order questions. The pre-service teachers in the study participated in the planned VR simulations and then reflected on their performance relative to each threshold concept. An interesting finding from this study was that the participation in the VR simulation, followed by reflection on performance, not only developed the sense of a collaborative shared experience, but it also supported pre-service teachers to develop their individual and collective teacher identity (Piro & O'Callaghan). While this study provides valuable information about the effectiveness of the VR simulation, a limitation of this study lies in the lack of emphasis and examination of the reflective process in supporting teacher identity development.

A significant component of professional socialization is reflective practice yet Ditchburn (2015) suggests that a traditional model of ITE practicum "does not encourage PSTs [pre-service teachers] themselves to theorize about their practice, engage in pedagogical risk taking, or to assimilate critical reflective practices as a considered and natural part of their work" (p. 94). In a study that explicitly targeted reflective practice, Ledger and Fischetti (2019) sought to identify the benefits and challenges of microteaching and VR simulations on pre-service teachers' self-efficacy in their preparation for practicum. Data were collected through observation of pre-service teachers teaching in the VR simulated environment, researcher engagement with literature, and a pre-simulation and post-placement questionnaire that was focused on capturing ITE reflections on preparedness. Participation in microteaching in a VR simulated environment was found to reinforce the importance of reflective practice by offering a preparatory tool for pre-service teachers to engage in the process, and by providing ITE lecturers with a potential diagnostic tool for early identification of the specific needs of pre-service teachers (Ledger & Fischetti, 2019). This is an important consideration for ITE, particularly in relation to the support of international students who are already having to adjust both psychologically and socio-culturally to the nuances of the Australian education system (Barton, Hartwig & Cain, 2015).

This current study adds to this emerging field of research by examining how a formal reflective task coupled with participation in a VR simulation can support international students' development of their teacher identity. Of specific interest was how international students' existing cultural identity was drawn on when reflecting on their teaching experience. In order to analyze this, we employed Rodgers' (2002) four functions of reflection as an analytical framework.

METHOD

A small-scale study that was conducted as part of a larger project that aimed to evaluate the effectiveness of a VR simulation to prepare pre-service teachers for the practicum experience is reported in this paper. The study reported in this paper is a sub-set of this wider project and focused on how international students' cultural identity is drawn on to reflect on teaching practice in a VR simulated classroom. The research question under investigation was: *How do international students enrolled in an initial teacher education course draw on their cultural identity to reflect on their teaching practice?*

The vehicle used to facilitate the online simulated classroom experience was a low-immersion virtual reality platform that draws on Mursion software to harness technology and human interaction in real-time. The VR simulation was embedded in the teacher education program of an Australian University in a third-year unit of work that examined diversity and equity in the primary/elementary school classroom. After engaging with various theoretical materials and policy documentation examining diversity and equity in a school-based context, PSTs were provided with a brief outlining the diverse needs of five school-aged students: Mina – a student with a diagnosis of ADD; Will – an extremely shy and quiet student with low self-esteem; Jayla – a happy and friendly student who has recently 'come out' publicly as homosexual; Emily – a student identified as gifted in reading and writing; and Carlos – a student with a diagnosis of ODD. PSTs were then required to plan to support these five children by developing a lesson plan that catered to diversity to teach in the VR simulated classroom. Once the lesson was planned, the PSTs were invited to share their lesson plans with the simulation specialists and book in a time to teach their lesson in the VR simulated classroom. On the day of the simulation, the PSTs logged into the simulated classroom from home or wherever they deemed suitable, and virtually delivered their lesson.

The simulation specialists are paid actors who controlled the actions of the student avatars in real-time. As the PSTs delivered their lessons, the simulation specialists were able to adapt the different student personas and engage in interactions that were immediate and responsive, reflecting a real-world teaching experience. Each simulated teaching session was recorded, and the simulation specialist sent a copy of the recording to the PSTs for later review and reflection. The PSTs were then required to draw on the theoretical materials presented in the diversity and equity unit of work to produce a 1000 word written reflection of their teaching practice with an explicit focus on how they supported culture, difference and diversity of need in their lesson.

The PSTs whose reflections were collected for this paper provided voluntary consent for their piece of work to be analyzed after the reflections had been assessed and graded. None of the researchers were involved in the teaching of the unit of work. Figure 1 provides a visual representation of the workings of the Mursion VR simulated classroom.

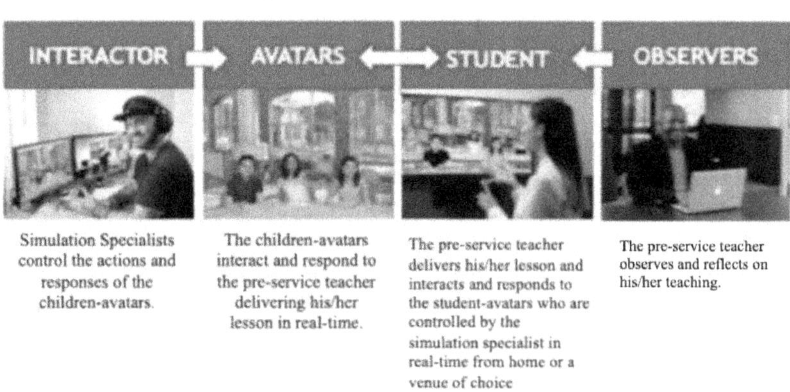

Figure 1. Components of the Mursion VR Simulated Classroom Experience (Adapted from Ledger 2017).

Sample and Data Analysis

Four third-year international PSTs' 1000 word written reflections of their teaching practice was taken as the sample data. The four third-year international PSTs in this study were all fulltime international students who had successfully completed two years of tertiary education in Australia as well as two face-to-face practicum experiences in Australian schools. PSTs who participated in the study disclosed that they were born overseas but did not disclose their country of origin. Each of the PSTs are referred to as PST1, PST2, PST3 and PST4.

Analysis of the written reflections was completed using Leximancer v4.5 with settings at default values, with the only exceptions set for the concept map explorer. The theme size was set at 53% to capture conceptually relevant themes and the visible concepts within the themes were set at 100% to ensure that the concepts were obvious to explain the lexical semantic themes.

Leximancer is ideal as an efficient tool that replicates the manual coding procedures used in content analysis to identify the underlying core themes and associations between themes (c.f., Smith & Humphreys, 2006). Being automated, it is free from the influence of human bias and/or expectation bias from a researcher's personal knowledge during the coding process, thereby removing issues such as coder reliability and subjectivity.

In broad terms, the algorithms within Leximancer identify and rank the themes by connectedness using the summed co-occurrence with all other themes. The algorithm begins at the top of the ranking and creates a theme group upon which it is centered. It then goes to the next ranked theme and either joins the nearest theme and adjusts the centroid of that theme (only if the next theme is near enough to any other theme group centroid on the map), or it starts a new theme group (Leximancer, 2018). Leximancer also generates a thematic summary that includes a connectivity score to indicate the relative importance of the themes, with the most important theme at 100% being found at the top. The subsequent grouping of themes enables the mapping of any relationships between the concepts. Finally, Leximancer produces a visualization of the thematic groupings and their associations with each other (Leximancer, 2018; Smith & Humphreys, 2006).

RESULTS

The Leximancer concept map as seen in Figure 2 represents five themes. There are three of dominant themes – STUDENTS, IN THE CLASSROOM, and LESSON, with two smaller themes of STORY AS A TOOL and SHARE. The three dominant themes are overlapped, which emphasizes the importance of a close relationship between these three themes. On the other hand, the smaller themes are quite far away with the SHARE theme being quite an outlier in the map.

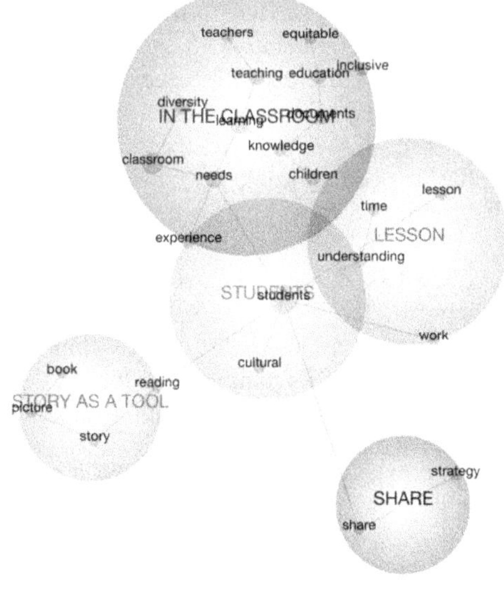

Figure 2. Leximancer concept map of four international students' reflections on their teaching practice and learning through the Mursian simulated classroom.

The central theme is STUDENTS that has 101 verbatim hits with two concepts of *experience* and *cultural* visible in the map. The visibility of the concept of "cultural" seems to suggest that the PSTs reflected meaningfully on how they responded to their own students' diversity or cultural background. For example, PST2 mentioned how they felt that they did not sufficiently prepare for their teaching to address their students' diverse needs.

> *However, due to my inadequate preparation and lack of effective teaching and behavior management strategies, I failed to promote equity and inclusion in my classroom. From this experience, I learnt that I need to plan as well as prepare resources carefully before each lesson – PST2*

Recognizing students' cultural nuances in the classroom teaching is seen as a way of extending a good experience, displaying some vigorous thinking in their own reflection.

The concept of "experience" is mentioned repeatedly by the PSTs as a way of responding to students' cultural and diverse needs. They viewed the experience they offered to their students through their teaching as being paramount to meet diverse needs in the classroom. PST4, for example, talked about modifying their approach in using stories to teach their students:

> *There are some adjustments that should be considered to make this learning experience more successful. Firstly, while I read the story, the students seem to be not focused and not engage in the story. Additionally, while reading, I should stop at some points to ask some questions such as "Have you shared any cookies with your family members?". This would have enhanced the students' understanding about the story content, as well as provided them with an opportunity to make a connection with their own experiences and invited their families' cultural practices into the classroom – PST4*

More importantly, the PSTs acknowledged that it is vital to think and implement classroom strategies that would encourage their students to have open and honest dialogue to help students to recognize and celebrate the differences and similarities between one another. At the same time, the PSTs reflected on their own cultural background and diversity that might impact on their own teaching of the students. PST2 mentioned in their reflection that "I need to think carefully about my own diversity and how I fit in to the classroom and how I can use my experiences to support my students."

Student "experience" as a concept is also clearly overlapping with other concepts that sit within the major theme of IN THE CLASSROOM that has 80 verbatim hits. This theme is considered major as it has the most comprehensive number of linking concepts that explain the four PSTs' emphasis in their reflections. The concepts that are visible and that are interconnected with experience are *classroom* being a *learning* space that is related to building the appropriate *knowledge* base in *children* from diverse backgrounds. The PSTs specifically referred to policy *documents* and frameworks such as the Australian Professional Standards for Teachers, the VIT Code of Conduct and Ethics as well as the Australian Curriculum as guiding principles for their *teaching* and their professional status as *teachers* – showing a connection to the teaching community. The PSTs also referred to such documents as providing them knowledge and basis on *inclusive* educational practices. For example, PST1 reflected that "Educational policy documentation gives instruction for the way in which practices should be undertaken, with the need to be supported by pedagogy that promotes inclusion and diversity in the classroom to foster an equitable learning environment". Along the same vein, PST4 mentioned in their reflection that "to consider an equity and diversity of teaching and expectations, an educator not only considers individual students' strengths and needs, but also the needs and strengths of the whole class."

The third theme is LESSON, which has a verbatim hit of 15. The smaller number of verbatim is concentrated around the concept of *lesson* planning that connects with concepts of *understanding, work* and *time*. The PSTs' reflections focus on how they plan their lessons taking into account students' ability to understand and learn. The PSTs clearly discuss how they work hard at engaging students into their lessons with careful planning of activities and associated activities. PST4 for example, shared that *"I applied a direct instruction approach for the body of the lesson. The students had a better understanding of the task because I broke down the steps and instructed them to do the next activity."* However, in reflecting their approaches, the PSTs also humbly noted the mistakes that they made in delivering their lessons. PST2 reflected that *"those tasks were not appropriately challenging and as a result, students lost interest and did not actively participate in the lesson."* Such humility and awareness signalled a reflective attitude that is important for the development of a teacher.

The fourth small theme is STORY AS A TOOL, a theme that shows how the PSTs reflected meaningfully on using stories as a tool. They understood that the stories are simply a means to an end and not an end in themselves. For example, PST2 mentioned that: "By not having the pictures, students could not draw on their own cultural backgrounds or family upbringings to visualize the story. If this was thought about carefully, I would have let them come into contact with the story in their own unique way."

The final and most distant theme is SHARE. The PSTs talked about two sides of sharing – sharing of their own cultural diversity with their students as a way of creating meaning and sharing between students as a strategy for learning in the classroom. For instance, PST4 mentioned that *"Coming from a cultural background where sharing food is an important part of my family, I was able to ensure that my own cultural background did not influence Carlos and that he felt safe to share his own cultural perspectives."* Whereas in their reflection, PST2 wrote how they *"planned opportunity for students to share their experiences and viewpoints with their classmates using think-pair-share strategy sharing in small groups or in pairs."*

DISCUSSION

Rodgers describes a four-phase reflective cycle that assists teachers to better understand student learning. Applying this cycle to pre-service teacher education provides a way to slow down the process of teaching and learning and support pre-service teachers to engage in extended forms of reflection and thinking (Rodgers,

2002). The incorporation of VR simulation further supports this process by providing both time and a safe space for pre-service teachers "to shift the weight of that thinking from their own teaching to their students' learning" and be present in the experience of learning about student learning (Rodgers, 2002, p.231). The pre-service teachers in this study showed a developing awareness of the cultural understandings of their own students and also in the sustained focus on student diversity. The pre-service teachers moved beyond the mechanics of teaching and towards an explicit focus on understanding the needs of students, including what students needed for effective learning. What was interesting in this study was that although pre-service teachers did not disclose their country of origin, they still drew heavily on their own cultural identity to reflect on and make sense of their teaching practice. This reflection involved identifying similarities between self and student and then providing alternative pedagogical approaches for moving forward. This suggests that the emergence of teacher identity is more than reconciling cultural identity within a new context but that it involves identifying a space in which difference can move together.

The incorporation of written reflection alongside the VR simulation proved an important resource to support pre-service teachers through the process of "telling the story of an experience" (Rodgers, 2002, p. 237). Rodgers suggested that "a prerequisite to being able to describe an experience is being able to distinguish between description (what one sees) and interpretation (ascribing meaning to what one sees)" (Rodgers, 2002, p.238). The written component embedded in the task provided pre-service teachers with a way to analyze and interpret their recorded teaching practice and reconcile their professional identity through "learning to take intelligent action" (Rogers, 2002, p. 235). This reflective piece was a crucial aspect of the pre-service teachers' learning as it shifted the onus of learning away from the lecturer and placed it squarely onto the pre-service teachers. The task also provided a way to actively engage pre-service teachers in the reflective process of theory and application.

Incorporating the practice of teaching into the university environment afforded the pre-service teachers in this study an opportunity to reflect deeply on their teaching by analyzing their experience and also their teaching practice. Being able to reflect is an important step toward the development of professional identity as it provides a safe space for pre-service teachers to experiment and perfect their craft. Having a safe space to think and connect to learning is particularly important for international students who are also learning about the Australian school context. It is a step that is elusive in the current model of school-based practicum experience and seen as paramount as a reflection of practice that connects with community needs (Rodgers, 2002).

CONCLUSION

The findings presented in this paper demonstrate that an immersive simulated teaching experience can support and enhance reflective practice among pre-service teachers. By giving the pre-service teachers an initial classroom experience within a controlled and repeatable format, it allowed the pre-service teachers to reflect on their practice in a systematic manner that echoed many of the criteria proposed by Rodgers (2002). This approach proved to be especially important for pre-service teachers from diverse backgrounds, as it enabled them to focus specifically on the way culture intersected with pedagogy and reflect on how their own cultural position might affect their teaching. VR systems such as the Mursion platform used for this study also provides university educators with an important diagnostic tool that can help identify gaps in support and are likely to become increasingly important as the ongoing impacts of COVID-19 continue to limit traditional practicum opportunities.

REFERENCES

Allen, J. (2008). *The theory-practice gap: Turning theory into practice in a pre-service teacher education program.* Unpublished PhD thesis, Central Queensland University.

Barton, G. M., Hartwig, K., & Cain, M. (2015). International students' experience of practicum in teacher education: An exploration through internationalisation and professional socialisation. *Australian Journal of Teacher Education, 40*(8), p.149-163.

Billingsley, G., Smith, S., Smith, S. & Meritt, J. (2019). A Systematic Literature Review of Using Immersive Virtual Reality Technology in Teacher Education. *Journal of Interactive Learning Research, 30*(1), 65-90.

Bryan, L., & Atwater, M. (2002). Teacher beliefs and cultural models: A challenge for science teacher preparation programs. *Science Education, 86*(6), 821–839. https://doi.org/10.1002/sce.10043

Cheng, L., Klinger, D. A., & Zheng, Y. (2007). The challenges of the Ontario Secondary School Literacy Test for second language students. *Language Testing, 24*(2), 185-208.

Chou, H. (2007). Multicultural teacher education: Toward a culturally responsible pedagogy. *Essays in Education, 21*, 139–162.

Collier, V. P., & Thomas, W. P. (1989). How quickly can immigrants become proficient in school English. *Journal of educational issues of language minority students, 5*(1), 26-38.

Cousik, R. (2015). Cultural and functional diversity in the elementary classroom: Strategies for teachers. *Journal for Multicultural Education, 9*(2), 54–67. https://doi.org/10.1108/JME-03-2015-0010

Darling-Hammond, L. (2016). Research on Teaching and Teacher Education and Its Influences on Policy and Practice. *Educational Researcher, 45*(2), 83–91. https://doi.org/10.3102/0013189X16639597

Dee, J. R., & Henkin, A. B. (2002). Assessing dispositions toward cultural diversity among preservice teachers. *Urban Education, 37*(1), 22-40.

Dickar, M. (2008). Hearing the silenced dialogue: An examination of the impact of teacher race on their experiences. *Race Ethnicity and Education, 11*(2), 115–132. https://doi.org/10.1080/13613320802110233

Elliman, J., Loizou, M, & Loizides, F. (2016). *Virtual Reality Simulation Training for Student Nurse Education in 2016 8th International Conference on Games and Virtual Worlds for Serious Applications* (VS-GAMES), S. 1–2.

Forrest, J., Lean, G., & Dunn, K. (2016). Challenging racism through schools: teacher attitudes to cultural diversity and multicultural education in Sydney, Australia. *Race Ethnicity and Education, 19*(3), 618–638. https://doi.org/10.1080/13613324.2015.1095170

Gan, Z. (2013). Learning to teach English language in the practicum: What challenges do non-native ESL student teachers face? *Australian Journal of Teacher Education, 38*(3), 6.

Gay, G. (2010). Acting on beliefs in teacher education for cultural diversity. *Journal of Teacher Education, 61*(1–2), 143–152. https://doi.org/10.1177/0022487109347320

Hammond, J. (2001). Literacies in school education in Australia: Disjunctions between policy and research. *Language and Education, 15*(2-3), 162-177.

Harford, J., & MacRuairc, G. (2008). Engaging student teachers in meaningful reflective practice. *Teaching and Teacher Education, 24*(7), 1884–1892. https://doi.org/10.1016/j.tate.2008.02.010

Harris, K., & Alexander, P. (1998). Integrated, Constructivist Education: Challenge and Reality. *Educational Psychology Review, 10*(2), 115–127. https://doi.org/10.1023/A:1022169018926

Hattie, J. (2009). *Visible learning: A synthesis of over 800 meta-analyses relating to achievement*: Routledge.

Horenczyk, G., & Tatar, M. (2002). Teacher's attitudes toward multiculturalism and their perceptions of the school organizational culture. *Teaching and Teacher Education, 18*(4), 435–445. https://doi.org/10.1016/S0742-051X(02)00008-2

Howard, J. (2010). The value of ethnic diversity in the teaching profession: A New Zealand case study. *International Journal of Education, 2*(1), 11. https://doi.org/10.5296/ije.v2i1.377

Janmaat, J. (2012). The effect of classroom diversity on tolerance and participation in England, Sweden and Germany. *Journal of Ethnic and Migration Studies, 38*(1), 21–39. https://doi.org/10.1080/1369183X.2012.640007

Khine, M., & Fisher, D. (2001). Classroom environment and teachers' cultural background in secondary science classes in an Asian context. Paper presented at the annual conference of the *Australian Association for Research in Education*, Perth, Australia.

Khine, M., & Fisher, D. (2004). Teacher interaction in psychosocial learning environments: Cultural differences and their implications in science instruction. International Journal of *Phytoremediation, 22*(1), 99–111. https://doi.org/10.1080/0263514042000187566

Konan, P., Chatard, A., Selimbegović, L., & Mugny, G. (2010). Cultural diversity in the classroom and its effects on academic performance: A cross-national perspective. *Social Psychology, 41*(4), 230–237. https://doi.org/10.1027/1864-9335/a000031

Ledger, S., & Fischetti, J. (2020). Micro-teaching 2.0: Technology as the classroom. *Australasian Journal of Educational Technology, 36*(1), 37-54. https://doi.org/10.14742/ajet.4561

Leximancer. (2018). *Leximancer user guide (Version 4.5)*. Leximancer.

Lindsey, J. (2004). Culture's role in teacher identity: Prompting teachers to explore their cultural background. *Action in Teacher Education, 25*(4), 9–13. https://doi.org/10.1080/01626620.2004.10648291

Lou, N., & Noels, K. (2020). Breaking the vicious cycle of language anxiety: Growth language mindsets improve lower-competence ESL students' intercultural interactions. *Contemporary Educational Psychology, 61*, p. 1-17, https://doi.org/10.1016/j.cedpsych.2020.101847

Loughran, J. (2010). *What expert teachers do: Enhancing professional knowledge*. Routledge.

Loughran, J., & Hamilton, M. (2016). Teaching and teacher education: The need to go beyond rhetoric. In R. Brandenberg, S. McDonough, J. Burke, & S.White (Eds.), *Teacher education: Innovation, intervention and impact*, (pp. 253-264) Springer.

McGarr, O. (2020). The use of virtual simulations in teacher education to develop pre-service teachers' behaviour and classroom management skills: Implications for reflective practice, *Journal of Education for Teaching*, 46:2, 159-169, DOI: 10.1080/02607476.2020.1724654

Phillipson, S. N., & Phillipson, S. (2020). *The power of expert teaching: Lessons for modern education.* Routledge.

Piro, J. S., & O'Callaghan, C. (2019) Journeying towards the profession: Exploring liminal learning within mixed reality simulations. *Action in Teacher Education*, 41(1), 79-95, DOI: 10.1080/01626620.2018.1534221

Rodgers, C. (2002). Defining reflection: Another look at John Dewey and reflective thinking. *Teachers college record, 104*(4), 842-866.

Schachner, M., Schwarzenthal, M., van de Vijver, F., & Noack, P. (2019). How all students can belong and achieve: Effects of the cultural diversity climate amongst students of immigrant and nonimmigrant background in Germany. *Journal of Educational Psychology, 111*(4), 703–716. https://doi.org/10.1037/edu0000303

Smith, A., & Humphreys, M. (2006). Evaluation of unsupervised semantic mapping of natural language with Leximancer concept mapping. *Behavior Research Methods, 38*(2), 262-279. doi:10.3758/BF03192778

Terenzini, P., Cabrera, A., Colbeck, C., Bjorklund, S., & Parente, J. (2001). Racial and Ethnic Diversity in the Classroom. *The Journal of Higher Education, 72*(5), 509–531. https://doi.org/10.1080/00221546.2001.11777112

Weisman, E. M., & Garza, S. A. (2002). Pre-service teacher attitudes toward diversity: Can one class make a difference? *Equity and Excellence in Education, 35*(1), 28–34. https://doi.org/10.1080/713845246

Wulandari, H. (2019). English teachers' cultural background and their teaching belief. *Lire Journal, 3*(1), 43–52. https://doi.org/10.33019/lire.v3i1.44

BIOGRAPHIES

Mark Finn, PhD, is a Senior Lecturer in Media and Communications. He was one of the first media scholars to explore the evolution of the World Wide Web as an emerging form of media, and has also published widely on various aspects of media evolution, including the historical development of electronic commerce and the social implications of mobile computing technologies. For the past seven years he has been specialising in growth and implications of computer games, and has published widely on the *Grand Theft Auto* series. His current work focuses mediatisation theory and explores the deepening impact media is having on a range of social institutions and relations. Email: mfinn@swin.edu.au

Sivanes Phillipson, PhD, is Swinburne University's Dean International and Professor of Education. She is also the Routledge Editor for Evolving Families Series, a series that focuses on issues, challenges and empirical best practices surrounding evolving families that impact upon their survival, development and outcomes. Sivanes' research interest and experience centres around teaching practices and parental engagement in early learning and care as the basis for children's formal learning and whole wellbeing. Her most recent work from an ARC Linkage is a resource website, www.numeracyathome.com that facilitates and enables parents and educators to engage in early mathematical learning. Her previous work includes the Australian Scholarship Groups Australia and New Zealand Parent Report Card project 2015-2017. The 2017 report has had extensive media outreach across the nation both in Australia and New Zealand. Email: sphillipson@swin.edu.au

Wendy Goff, PhD, has worked closely with schools to develop a variety of intervention and support programs targeting the educational and social welfare needs of children and families. Her research focuses on adult relationships. She is particularly interested in how adults might come together to support the learning and development of children. Throughout her career, Wendy has worked as a pre-school teacher, a primary school teacher, and a social welfare worker. She joined the tertiary setting in 2010 and teaches in the secondary, primary and early childhood teacher education programs. Email: wgoff@swin.edu.au

Peer-Reviewed Article
Special Edition | Reflection and Reflective Thinking

© *Journal of International Students*
Volume 10, Issue S2 (2020), pp. 86-100
ISSN: 2162-3104 (Print), 2166-3750 (Online)
ojed.org/jis

International Students' Reflections on Employability Development Opportunities During a One-Year Masters-level Program in the UK

Omolabake Fakunle
University of Edinburgh, Scotland

Anne Pirrie
University of the West of Scotland

ABSTRACT

This article explores reflection and reflective thinking, drawing upon qualitative research on international students' perceptions of developing their employability while studying in the UK. It addresses a gap in the literature by making a connection between internationalization and employability, concepts that are mainly framed as separate discursive realms. The literature on internationalization is focused around international student recruitment and the benefits to the host institution; the employability discourse is oriented towards national policies on the development of human capital through home students in the domestic market. The reflective thinking demonstrated by the international students illustrates the challenges they faced in seeking opportunities to enhance their employability within and outside the university; and to (re)assess learning opportunities that are integrated with work experience. The findings suggest that there is scope for embedding employment development opportunities (EDOs) at a systemic level in order to enhance the experience of international students.

Keywords: internationalization, employability, international students, work-integrated learning, employment development opportunities

The internationalization agenda has given rise to the presence of large numbers of international students on university campuses across the UK. Despite the availability of data on student numbers collected by national agencies, (e.g. the Higher

Educational Statistics Agency (HESA) in the UK and supranational organisations such as the OECD), there are concerns about the lack of insight into international students' employability (Huang et al., 2014). In the UK context, this gap can be linked to a lack of alignment of internationalization and employability discourses. The literature on internationalization is framed around international student recruitment and the associated benefits to the host institutions/countries (Lomer, 2018). In contrast, the employability discourse is oriented towards developing the skills and knowledge of home students (Tomlinson, 2008; Tymon, 2013) as part of a human capital driven national policy (Yorke, 2004). As Gillies (2015, p.1) notes, the human capital perspective "[promotes] education as an "investment" which yields returns in due course to the individual in terms of pay and to the state in terms of employment and economic growth". The theory is encapsulated and expressed in the definition of employability as developing knowledge, skills and attitudes to improve the likelihood of obtaining and retaining fulfilling work (Hillage & Pollard, 1998). This underpins the focus on employability in quantitative and qualitative terms and the role of higher education to produce employable graduates. The employability narrative in the UK is operationalized by the HESA. Prior to 2017, HESA used the Destinations of Leavers from Higher Education survey that captured the numbers of graduates in employment six months after finishing their studies in UK universities, as a measure of employability. These data excluded international students. The new HESA Graduate Outcomes survey was initiated in 2017/18 and the first report released in June 2020 did not include specific employability-related data on non-European international students. It remains unclear how future employability-related policy will take account of the impact of the Covid-19 pandemic.

However, universities around the world, including in the UK, aim to recruit students from a global pool and to 'produce' graduates who are prepared to live and work in a global world, under the banner of an internationalization agenda. Research has shown that the prospect of enhanced employability is a key driver for international students studying abroad (Archer, 2016; Fakunle, 2020; Nilsson & Ripmeester, 2016). This article brings these discrete policy discourses into alignment and explores the tensions between them by focusing on the reflections of international students (Fakunle, 2019a). As Fakunle (2019b) and Page and Chahboun (2019) have pointed out, the voices of international students are largely absent from the relevant research literature.

In marked contrast to the UK, Bennett and Ferns (2017) point out the employability of international students has been high on the research agenda in Australia. There the focus has been on the importance of work integrated learning (WIL) (Gribble et al., 2015; Tran & Soejatminah, 2017). However, as Gribble et al. (2015) point out there is a gap between the promise of employability development, opportunities advertised, and lived experience for international students. In the UK context, there remains a gap in understanding how and to what extent international students engage with WIL. This article examines these gaps, drawing on a study that explored the perceptions of international students on developing their employability during a one-year Masters-level study abroad (Fakunle, 2019a). The focus is on how international students from a range of countries demonstrated their capacities for reflection and reflective thinking about the opportunities related to enhanced employability during their study abroad experience. It includes the extent to which their lived experience met these expectations of employability. The findings discussed in this paper raise the need for HEIs to support international student employability during their study abroad, specifically in relation to the opportunities (or lack of opportunities) to undertake work placement during their study abroad, and the implications for their future career trajectories.

REFLECTIVE PRACTICE IN HIGHER EDUCATION

Barton & Ryan (2017) note it is difficult to define reflective thinking, as what is deemed to constitute a reflective act or practice partly depends on context. These authors highlight key aspects of reflection expected of learners in higher education, in relation to students' experience of assessment; feedback; and work integrated learning (WIL) (see Barton & Ryan, 2017). They also noted that "despite its importance, reflection is not well implemented or undertaken, particularly in regard to explicit support for culturally diverse students and their supervisors" (p. 106). The importance accorded to reflection in discourse relating to higher education brings to the fore scholarly interest in how international students from non-western countries adjust to a different culture of teaching and learning. Much of the research in this area has focused on the lack of critical thinking of Chinese students in western universities from an academic perspective (Durkin, 2008; O'Sulivan & Guo, 2010). However, the examination of Chinese literature shows that reflective thinking is present in Confucian culture (Tian & Low, 2011). Empirical research also shows that Chinese students studying in the west demonstrate critical and reflective thinking (Fakunle et. al., 2016; Kingston & Forland, 2008). Fakunle et al. (2016, p. 33) found that the Chinese students in their study struggled to understand the assessment requirement to show 'evidence of critical thinking'. The feedback from their first semester assignment served as a "trigger event" (Brookfield, 1987) for all six participants to reflect on their understanding. The findings revealed the differing perceptions of students in terms of how they perceived the development of critical thinking in their academic work.

In contrast, there is relatively little research in relation to international students' engagement in reflective practice in relation to the workplace components of their programs. Barton and Hartwig (2017) highlight the need for "systemic change within higher education institutions [HEIs] related to work placements and international students" as part of an integrated approach towards embedding employability in internationalization (p. 10). While it is crucial to understand practice related to work placements for international students (Barton & Hartwig, 2017), it is also important to ascertain the extent to which international students perceive opportunities for WIL to be embedded in their programs. As will be discussed, Rodgers' (2002) four criteria of reflection capture international students' reflections on the extent to which they had access to EDOs within and outside the institution. Drawing on the work of Dewey (1933), Rodgers (2002) identified four criteria to illuminate the process as well as the purpose of reflection, which was regarded as a meaning-making process; as a rigorous way of thinking, as important in and for community; and as set of attitudes. As Rodgers (2002, p. 844) argued, the main purpose of reflection is to "derive meaning from experience" Similarly, we believe it is important to understand the reflections of international students in relation to how they make sense of a particular aspect of their experience, namely employability development opportunities (EDOs) during study abroad. The central question this article addresses is: How did the international students in the study reported below reflect on the wider implications of the absence of WIL opportunities?

SETTING THE SCENE

For the purpose of this article, international students are defined based on domiciliation, that is, they are resident in the UK for study purposes. The qualitative research upon which we draw below was conducted at one of the top five recruiting institutions for international students in the UK. The purposive selection of participants (Maxwell, 2013) made possible variability in the sample and inclusion of students from China and India (the biggest exporters of international students) and nine other countries (Canada, Columbia, Mexico, Nigeria, Singapore, South Africa, Taiwan, Turkey, and the US). Ethical approval for the study was granted by the university. To guide the focus of the research, a pilot study was conducted involving three students from two of the selected programmes. The participants (n=19; 4 males and 15 females) were recruited from four programs in four schools (Education; Business; Literatures; Languages and Cultures; and Social and Political Studies) in the university with the highest numbers of international students at the time the study was conducted. Two rounds of face-to-face semi-structured interviews (n =36) were conducted with the participants over the course of the one-year Master's program, at the end of the first and second semesters respectively. The specific programs are not identified (thereafter named as Programs 1 to 4) to ensure anonymity of the participants, and the names of all the students have been changed. The gender of the participants largely reflects the student cohort, for example, Program 1 did not have any male students enrolled when the study was conducted. For this article, we do not focus on demographics, such as, country of origin or gender. Rather, we focus on the shared characteristic of these international students as non-citizens in the host country because, as will be discussed, this singular factor had the greatest influence on how international students perceived the employability development opportunities afforded to them during study abroad. In other words, challenges around the affordances of EDOs in the host environment resonated with all participants, regardless of the variability of their country of origin.

All interviews were audio recorded and fully transcribed. The interviews were analysed thematically (Braun & Clarke, 2006) using NVivo. Member checking was used to ensure the trustworthiness of the coded data into themes and categories. In this article, we focus on themes that emerged from the participants' narratives that capture and illustrate international students' perceptions of the work-integrated learning (WIL) opportunities afforded to them. These ranged from compulsory short-term (i.e. up to one week) individual industrial placements with the option of an additional placement secured by the students themselves (Program 1); to longer placements with a research component and dissertation, with work-based mentors and academic supervisors (Program 2); and short-term group work experience placement in a company in Italy (Program 3). WIL was not offered as part of the course in Program 4.

The findings presented below highlight variations in access to EDOs across four different Masters-level programs in a UK university. Invariably, the international students who participated in the study reflected on the extent to which they had access to EDOs within and outside the institution. Rodgers' (2002) criteria for reflection are of relevance here: first as a meaning-making process, as international students consider how their main motivation for studying abroad, that is, to enhance their employability, connects with their experience. Rodgers describes the second criterion as a rigorous way of thinking. This recalls Dewey's definition of education: "that reconstruction or reorganisation of experience which adds to the meaning of experience and which increases [one's] ability to direct the course of subsequent experience" (cited in Rodgers, 2002, p. 848). By making sense of the [taught and practical] components of their study, the participants needed to reassess their experience and what it meant to them, in order to assess the implications for further steps. As Rodgers noted, whilst meaning can be created in isolation, richer meanings can be derived from experience in community. This relates to Rodgers' third criterion namely as being important in and for community. The school/ program and the university constitute the immediate community for international students, as EDOs are linked to provision such as WIL embedded in courses. The wider community is relevant to facilitate WIL (such as work placements) conducted with organizations outside the university, or part-time work sourced by the students, as in Program 1. Rodgers (2002) deems a set of attitudes as the fourth criterion for reflection. Based on experience within the school community, this affective aspect of reflection could influence whether students express a positive or negative response to learning. Going back to Dewey, Rodgers (2002) points out that human attitudes fall into two categories: to see what we wish to see, rather than accept the evidence before us, or to believe the worst even if unsubstantiated. Below we draw on interviews with participants in order to illustrate their capacity for reflection under the following themes: seeking employability development opportunities within and outside the university; and (re)assessment of WIL.

International Students' Meaning-Making Reflections on Employability Development Opportunities

The meaning-making reflective process (Rodgers, 2002) demonstrated by the participants started before they embarked on their study abroad. The school website listed information regarding the different types of WIL embedded in the selected programs. Congruent with findings from a large-scale survey of international students (ICEF Monitor, 2019) the participants cited the institutional website as the main source of information about the program, including the EDOs they expected to engage in as a part of their study experience. For example, Adele (a student from Canada) explained what had attracted her to Program 2:

> The work-based dissertation was something that drew me to this
> program because then you have a chance to network with different

organizations when you're writing your dissertation and hopefully make contacts instead of just getting a sociology degree and being like, I have this now, somebody just hire me.

Adele's remarks are illustrative of the international students' accounts across different programs where WIL was embedded in the course of study. Adele did not respond to repeated invitations to attend the second interview held at the end of the second semester. Based on the discussions during the first interview, it was assumed that she had returned home to seek work opportunities which she had said were not available, as she had hoped. Her actions suggested an attempt at "reconstructing or reorganizing experience" of the reflection process (Rodgers, 2002, p. 855) as the international students made sense of their experience in planning their future steps.

As noted by Barton and Ryan (2017), processes of reflection can be triggered at different times depending on new encounters or issues. Similarly, in the context under study, the reflective processes were not linear for students across all four programs. For some of the international students in the study reported here, a fundamental factor accounting for a lack of participation in WIL was a lack of inclusion in the program. The absence of a practical WIL opportunity was another trigger for reflection. Of interest here is Rodgers' (2002) third criterion of reflection, that is, interaction with others in the community. Fang (a student from China on Program 4) discussed interest in work experience with a tutor. The tutor was supportive and provided guidance for her to secure a short-term volunteering position with an organization that specialized in learning technology for children. In line with her educational "quest" to attain her future goals, Fang demonstrated a resilient attitude that fits Rodgers' notion of reflection as "attitudes that value the personal and intellectual growth of oneself" (p. 845). The participants talked at length about their keen awareness of the value of WIL, including another student on Program 4, Indira (India) who pleaded for a "rounded education":

If given an opportunity I will like to tell them [the school] that please, have some kind of internship [WIL] in place for the students. Because Masters program is something that the internship could add value to. The benefit of that is that you get to work in an environment, and you can relate it to what you are studying. It gives you a more rounded effect.

Abby (USA) described the benefits of WIL offered in Program 1:

The strength of the Masters program is its applied practice component, which gives students the ability to work in real-world situations and learn from industry partners. After working with multiple festivals and film exhibition bodies in Scotland, I felt prepared enough to apply for a traineeship [internship] in film distribution in New York City. That I successfully got the job is a testament, in my opinion, to what I've been able to do this past year. So, I feel like my current study experience is not only relevant to my aspirations, but vital to them.

The comments made by Abby encapsulate Rodgers' (2002) four criteria of reflection as: a meaning-making process (recognising the strength of the master's program, pre-enrolment and during study experience); as a rigorous way of thinking (analytic approach linking the master's to initial WIL and incremental work experience (internship) in both national and international contexts); in interaction with others (working with others); and attitudes and values (initiative and personal attributes to commit to pursuit and achievement of current and future goals). Abby's comments about satisfaction with the program resonated with comments from other students in Program 1, as well as two students in Program 3; Bond, (Singapore) and Yin (Taiwan) who were selected to participate in a week-long WIL opportunity.

Across all four programs, it was found that international students demonstrated reflection regarding the EDOs within and outside their schools. This meaning-making process occurred prior to their arrival and is evidenced in activities such as consulting the university website and selecting the program that best fitted their future career goals. Further on during their study, in the case where WIL was unavailable (Program 4), the students sought alternative work experience options, such as volunteering. They demonstrated commitment to their personal and intellectual growth which are attitudes captured in the reflective process (Rodgers, 2002). However, despite their keen interest, the lack of access to WIL was found to be a major barrier to enhancing EDOs. We now turn our attention to how international students (re)assessed the WIL opportunities during their study abroad.

(RE)ASSESSMENT OF WORK INTEGRATED LEARNING OPPORTUNITIES

Rodgers (2002) stated that "Dewey was acutely aware of the need to slow down the interval between thought and action" (p. 852). For international students, this suggests that they would benefit from a reassessment of their expectations and access to work experience (whether WIL or other types of work experience) during their study abroad. For the study participants, meaning-making processes were reassessed in the light of the opportunities and the barriers they faced with regards to their work prospects. This reassessment occurred mainly after the international students had checked the work opportunities, including part-time work, internships and volunteering positions advertised on the Careers Service website. Five out of the 19 participants engaged in part-time work unrelated to their master's program. Mariana (Colombia) and Jackie (USA) worked as waitresses. Sofia (Colombia) did some babysitting. Indira (India) and Bola (Nigeria) both worked for one day. In the case of Indira, she participated in a one-day university-run event. Bola did a social worker job and quit after one day. She described the job as more like a full-time job, and she reasoned that she could not cope with her studies and the demands of the job. Except for Indira and Bola, the participants who engaged in part-time jobs said this was primarily a way to augment their living costs while studying abroad. The rigour and the short length (one-year) of doing the master's was cited as a deterrent from seeking part-time work. As Lan (China) puts it, "the most realistic reason is because I pay my tuition fees for this program so I must study hard to learn knowledge well. To not make my money wasted."

However, as the brief narrative below shows, Mariana added some important points related to doing part-time work:

My mum pays for my accommodation…The part-time work is to help my mum with the expenses because it is expensive to live here… I also think having a job helps you to kind of organise yourself. You manage your time wisely as you know that I have to work these days, so I have to have these days to study. So, it gives you discipline. And you know I like the fact that it allows you to meet people outside the university. You can switch your brain off and talk to normal people. It is a bit like you are always talking about your life and about theoretical stuff. Then at work you are like a normal person talking about the weather and I really like the people from my job. They are like really real people and I really like them. So it is like another social sphere. That is good to have as well. To escape from Uni I go to work.

Mariana's reflections above demonstrate an awareness of the benefits of part-time work as a way of developing employability related skills, such as, organisation skills and time management. She also raises the benefits of having time out from her studies to relate with people outside the university. These external opportunities for work experience could help international students to develop intercultural and interpersonal skills.

Abby (USA) did an internship in her home country. This demonstrated her keen interest in internships and resourcefulness to seek an EDO outside her host country. The participants, however, cited the lack of internships as a major issue. For example, Yin (Taiwan) shared details of her pursuit of a summer internship in another European Union (EU) country and how she was denied because the recruiter said she was not from an EU country. Based on their experience, international students cited two main reasons for their inability to undertake internships. Both reasons directly linked to their status as international students. The first reason was the student visa that provided a limited right to work. This meant that they could not undertake an internship during term time that exceeded the 20-hour permitted time to work. This highlighted inequities in internship opportunities during study period, as this was not an issue for their peers who were not international students. The second point related to a lack of interest by employers in recruiting international students, which Chao (China) and Fang (China) recounted as their experience when they attended the Careers Fair organised at the host institution. It seems ironic that Careers Fairs are organised for all students, however, it is unclear how international students are benefitting from such events if their status and affordances at the host community limits their access to EDOs during their study.

Whilst 11 students engaged in volunteering activities, Bola (Nigeria) reiterated the need for volunteering opportunities to be relevant to future career goals:

Whatever I have to volunteer for has to add knowledge and experience in my field of study. I am not a young scholar. I am an adult learner. Any moment for me now is valuable. I can't just waste it. I want focused experience and not scattered experience. I want something that will earn me an advantage. Like, whoa you got this experience in the UK! Not gaining experience cleaning the environment in the UK, because, if I want to work in high profile establishment it does not add up.

Narratives of the international students discussed so far provide snapshots of their reflection and reflective practice regarding their experiences and their meaning making through the challenges they faced. We will draw on the experience of one of the participants (Harshad) to illustrate the meaning-making processes of reflection over the course of the one-year master's study.

Harshad (India), a 22-year old student in Program 3 provided a cogent example of how international students re-assessed the work-placement opportunities, or the lack thereof, during their study experience. During the first interview, in the first few months after arrival in the UK, Harshad seemed very enthusiastic about the potential work opportunities afforded to him by studying abroad:

> I have checked the website of the companies I want to apply to in the UK. I am in the first stage of the application process right now. I am applying for jobs. The biggest challenge is since I am an international student I require a visa to work over here and it is not very easy to get that. There are very few organisations who are willing to sponsor candidates and we need to express ourselves very well to try and get that visa. You have put in a lot of money and you want to have a good job. It's a hard situation. But since they are hiring the best I think it's alright. Not a big challenge. The chances are very bright. Very bright.

However, during the second interview, Harshad provided a clear illustration of how "one moves from an impressionistic sense to an articulated idea" (Rodgers, 2002, p. 854). By the end of the second semester, Harshad's optimism about work opportunity had dwindled considerably:

> At first, my intention was to work in the UK for a couple of years then to go back to India. I heard that it's difficult. But getting a job is not easy in any part of the world so I said let's give it a try but when I came here, and I started applying it's almost impossible. The visa regulation makes it very difficult for us to get work in the UK. The organizations are not willing to sponsor non-EU people. A lot of organizations don't even consider the application. That makes me feel disappointed. It was always rejection at the very first stage in the online application. I get email in a couple of hours or the next day that my application cannot be processed to the next stage. EU people don't need visas, so they are progressing to the next stage. They have interviews. They are progressing nicely. The job market here is not in our [non-EU students] favour right now.

Based on his lived experience, Harshad revealed a deep understanding of systematic obstacles that undermined his efforts to secure work experience in the UK. In his case, these issues centred around the visa system in the UK. Some organizations may not have been UK Visa and Immigration (UKVI) licensed sponsors, which meant that they could not offer employment to non-EU nationals. UKVI-licensed sponsors need to pay administrative costs to employ non-EU citizens. The additional costs and resource implications of recruiting non-EU students are likely to deter employers. A caveat is warranted here. Brexit (the UK leaving the EU) means that visa policies for EU students are likely to change in the next few years. Furthermore, in 2020, changes to visa rules in the UK have seen the re-introduction of a two-year post-study work visa for international students. It remains to be seen how the changes in the visa policy will impact upon opportunities for international students to gain work experience.

Harshad's experience was not unique. Across the four programs, the participants cited several instances where individual attempts to seek part-time work and internship opportunities were thwarted. The main reason for the rejection of their application by employers was due to their status as international students. This points to one of the systemic flaws in the internationalization agenda, such as, issues around equality of access and the human rights of international students in the host country (Marginson, 2012). A lack of equality of access to work experience can be seen to deviate from what Dewey considers as the purpose of education for "intellectual, moral, and emotional growth of the individual and consequently, the evolution of democratic society" (Rodgers, 2002, p. 845). On the one hand, internationalization is an evolution of higher education society beyond national borders. As universities seek to internationalize, the student community has become more diverse. Yet it remains to be seen whether the internationalization agenda reflects the values of a democratic society in respect to equality of access, for example, to work opportunities. This question is important when considering the expectations of international students like Harshad who have expectations that studying abroad will equip them with the skills to live and work in a global world. This is how Harshad described the situation:

> Today is a globalized world. If you want to work at a global level you need to understand different cultures, different perspectives. You need to understand how decision is made in different cultures. The organizations are working in global level and if you want work for an organization at the global level you need to understand how the process works.

Harshad was able to intellectualize the challenges related to a lack of opportunity to undertake a work experience. This was in marked contrast to his emotional response to questions during the first interview about work opportunities during study abroad. He created meaning out of his experience as part of a reflective process, along the lines proposed by Rodgers (2002). However, this meaning-making was not unproblematic. Having identified the problem, a great sense of relief at the stage of the reflective process (Rodgers, 2002) was lacking. Rather, Harshad evoked a sense of resignation. When asked about what support he expected from the university Harshad said:

> I don't see the role of the university because the visa rules are formed by the government. And organizations have to stick to it. The university is obviously helping us to apply. They are willing to review our CVs. These things are more in the hands of government or organizations.

Here Harshad showed a sense of disappointment and resignation as he could not see a path to work experience abroad. He reasoned that the support from the university was insufficient for him to access the work experience he wanted. He displayed a reflective attitude, in so far as he noted that different stakeholders, including the government, organizations, and the university, have different roles regarding the EDOs available to him.

It is important to recognize that like many of his peers Harshad's main criticisms were reserved for non-academic dimensions of university life, such as support services, rather than individual members of the academic staff. The tenor of these international students' observations about the deficiencies in their engagement with the careers service, for example, echoed the findings from the study by Arambewela and Maringe (2012). These authors stressed the need for universities to develop systems and support that are effective towards addressing the problems and challenges faced by international students. There has not been scope here to give an account of the type of dialogic encounters with faculty that international students on all four programs reported. For now, it will suffice to note that these lend further weight to the findings from other research to the effect that support from lecturers and tutors enhances the experience of international students (Lacina, 2002; Tran, 2008).

CONCLUSION

Our focus here has been on the reflections of international students on the WIL aspects of their study, as a means of furthering their legitimate career aspirations before embarking upon their studies. We drew attention to the best possible scenarios for international students who undertook programs with integrated WIL. We explored the challenges faced by some international students in attempting to secure a placement in situations where this was not a compulsory aspect of a program. Several demonstrated considerable resourcefulness and tenacity in seeking other opportunities to develop their employability. The international students who participated in the study reported here raised issues around a lack of equal access to part-time work opportunities in the host country, echoing the findings of other studies that examined issues around international students' employability. The progressive disillusionment of Harshad casts a long shadow. The brief snapshot of this case that we were able to present here underlines the fact that "reflection requires cognitive discipline [and] calls upon an individual's emotional discipline" (Rodgers, 2002, p. 863). Like many of his peers, Harshad remained "engaged in the experience as it [was] happening, in an undistracted way, so that data can be gathered through observation (whole-heartedness and directness)" (Rodgers, 2002, p. 863). His willingness to remain open-minded and to entertain many interpretations of his experience in order not to limit his understanding is apparent from the extracts of the interview transcript presented above. His case eloquently demonstrates that "one must accept that a shift in understanding of an experience may call for an entire shift in outlook" (Rodgers, 2002, p. 864).

The results of this study were evident in the international students' reflections on their experience through a meaning-making process and rigorous intellectual exercise. Their interpretation of their experience culminated in action, or in some cases in a realization of the limitations of individual agency. It is clear that the responsibility for enhancing employability among the international student population does not lie solely with the students themselves. The interview data indicate that support from staff was crucial towards facilitating relevant WIL projects. Yet it remains the case that not all students were successful in terms of achieving their desired outcomes. It is not possible here to do justice to the human and financial costs associated with this loss. The diverse experiences of international students suggest that there are gaps in provision that need to be examined and addressed. In agreement with recent studies in this area (Barton & Ryan, 2017; Goodwin & Mbah, 2019), there is a clear need for universities to implement support systems to address the problems and challenges international students face to access EDOs during their study abroad.

We recognise that the ameliorative intentions expressed above align with the second criterion for reflection identified by Rodgers (2002), namely a rigorous way of thinking that recalls a definition of education: "that reconstruction or reorganisation of experience which adds to the meaning of experience and which increases [one's] ability to direct the course of subsequent experience" (cited in Rodgers, 2002, p. 848). And yet, tinkering with the engine will not enable us to address adequately the consequences of the fundamental dichotomy to which we drew readers' attention at the beginning of this article. The dichotomy is between the internationalization agenda on the one hand, with its relentless focus of furthering the interests of the institutions whose business model is based on international recruitment, and the legitimate aspirations of the international students who embrace opportunities to study abroad as a means of enhancing their employment prospects in the long term. At the time of writing, it seems that the legacy of the COVID-19 pandemic may lead to a fundamental reassessment of a business model founded on international recruitment. The assumption that there is an international market for online learning that will partially compensate for international students' inability or reluctance to take up places on master's degree courses abroad seems open to question. If nothing else, it exposes a profound and deep-rooted systemic failure to recognise the legitimate career aspirations of international students who are well versed in the art of reflective practice.

REFERENCES

Arambewela, R., & Maringe, F. (2012). Mind the gap: staff and postgraduate perceptions of student experience in higher education. *Higher Education Review. 44*(2), 63-84.

Archer, W. (2016). *International taught postgraduate students: The UK's competitive advantage.* London: HE International Unit.

Barton, G. M., & Hartwig, K. (2017). The importance of positive intercultural exchanges for international students on work placements in higher education. In G. M. Barton & M. Ryan (Eds.), *Professional learning in the workplace for international students: Exploring theory and practice,* (pp. 3-12*).* Springer.

Barton, G. M., & Ryan, M. (2017). Reflection and reflective practice for international students and their supervisors in context. In G. M. Barton & K.

Hartwig. (Eds.), *Professional learning in the workplace for international students: Exploring theory and practice,* (pp. 93-110). Springer.

Bennett, D., & Ferns, S. (2017). Functional and cognitive aspects of employability: implications for international students. In G. M. Barton & K. A. Hartwig. (Eds.), *professional learning in the workplace for international students: Exploring theory and practice,* (pp. 203-224). Springer.

Braun, V., & Clarke, V. (2006) Using thematic analysis in psychology. *Qualitative Research in Psychology, 3*(2), 77–101.

Brookfield, S. (1987). *Developing critical thinkers: Challenging adults to explore alternative ways of thinking and acting.* Open University Press.

Dewey, J. (1933). *How we think.* Prometheus Books.

Durkin, K. (2008). The adaptation of East Asian master's students to western norms of critical thinking and argumentation in the UK. *Intercultural Education, 19,* 15-27. https://doi.org/10.1080/14675980701852228

Fakunle, O. (2020) Developing a framework for international students' rationales for studying abroad, beyond economic factors. *Policy Futures in Education* https://doi.org/10.1177/1478210320965066.

Fakunle, O. (2019a). *International student perceptions on studying abroad and developing employability during a UK Masters* (Unpublished doctoral dissertation). The University of Edinburgh.

Fakunle, O. (2019b). 18 June. Empowering the student voice in internationalisation. *World Education News +Reviews.* https://wenr.wes.org/2019/06/empowering-the-student-voice-in-internationalization

Fakunle, L., Allison, P. & Fordyce, K. (2016). Chinese postgraduate students' perspectives on developing critical thinking on a UK Education Masters. *Journal of Curriculum and Teaching, 5*(1), 27-38. http://dx.doi.org/10.5430/jctv5n1p27

Gillies D. (2015). Human capital theory in education. In: Peters M. (Ed.) *Encyclopaedia of Educational Philosophy and Theory.* Springer, Singapore. https://doi.org/10.1007/978-981-287-532-7_254-1

Goodwin, K., & Mbah, M. (2019). Enhancing the work placement experience of international students: towards a support framework, *Journal of Further and Higher Education, 43*(4), 521-532.

Gribble, C., Blackmore, J., & Rahimi, M. (2015). Challenges to providing work integrated learning to international business students at Australian universities. *Higher Education, Skills and Work-Based Learning, 5*(4), 401-416.

Kingston, E. & Forland, H. (2008). Bridging the gap in expectations between international students and academic staff. *Journal of Studies in International Education,* 12, 204–221.

Huang, R., Turner, R. & Chen, Q. (2014). Chinese international students' perspective and strategies in preparing for their future employability. *Journal of Vocational Education and Training, 66*(2), 175-193.

Hillage, J. & Pollard, E. (1998). *Employability: Developing a framework for policy analysis.* Department for Education and Employment.

ICEF Monitor (2019). *Stealth applicants and the role of the institutional website.* https://monitor.icef.com/2019/10/stealth-applicants-and-the-role-of-the-institutional-website/.

Lacina, J. G. (2002). Preparing international students for a successful social experience in higher education. *New Directions for Higher Education 117,* (1), 21-27.

Lomer, S. (2018). UK policy discourses and international student mobility: The deterrence and subjectification of international students. *Globalisation, Societies and Education, 16*(3), 308-324. https://doi.org/10.1080/14767724.2017.1414584

Marginson, S. (2012). Including the other: Regulation of the human rights of mobile students in a nation-bound world. *Higher Education 63,* 497-512.

Maxwell, J. A. (2013). *Qualitative research design: An interactive approach.* Los Angeles: Sage.

Nilsson, P. A., & Ripmeester, N. (2016). International student expectations: career opportunities and employability. *Journal of International Students, 6*(2), 614-631.

O'Sullivan, M. & Guo, L. (2010). Critical thinking and Chinese international students: An East-West dialogue. *Journal of Contemporary Issues in Education, 5,* 53-73.

Page, A. G. & Chahboun, S. (2019). Emerging empowerment of international students: How international student literature has shifted to include the students' voices. *Higher Education, 78*(5), 871-885. https://doi.org/10.1007/s10734-019-00375-7

Rodgers, C. (2002). Defining reflection: Another look at John Dewey and reflective thinking. *Teachers College Record, 104*(4), 842–866.

Tian, J. & Low, G. D. (2011). Critical thinking and Chinese university students: A review of the evidence. *Language, Culture and Curriculum, 24*(1), 61-76. https://doi.org/10.1080/07908318.2010.546400

Tomlinson, M. (2008). 'The degree is not enough': Students' perceptions of the role of higher education credentials for graduate work and employability. *British Journal of Sociology of Education, 29*(1), 49–61. https://doi.org/10.1080/01425690701737457

Tran, L. T. (2008). Unpacking academic requirements: international students in management and education disciplines. *Higher Education Research and Development, 27*(3), 245-256. https://doi.org/10.1080/07294360802183804

Tran, L. T. & Soejatminah, S. (2017). Integration of work experience and learning for international students: From harmony to inequality. *Journal of Studies in International Education, 21*(3), 261-277. doi: 10.1177/1028315316687012

Tymon, A. (2013). The student perspective on employability. *Studies in Higher Education, 38*(6), 841-856. https://doi.org/10.1080/03075079.2011.604408

Yorke, M. (2004). Employability in the undergraduate curriculum: some student perspectives. *European Journal of Education, 39*(4), 409-427. https://doi.org/10.1111/j.1465-3435.2004.00194.x

BIOGRAPHIES

Omolabake Fakunle, PhD, is a Teaching Fellow and Coordinator of the MSc Education General Pathway at the University of Edinburgh. She is a Fellow of Higher Education Academy (FHEA). She is Advisory Board Member, Journal of Comparative and International Higher Education, and Co-convenor, Scottish Educational Research Association ECR Network. Her award-winning research explores the intersections of internationalisation, student experience, employability and education policy. Omolabake has led and worked in multi-disciplinary teams on national and multi-national research projects on student experience in higher education. She shares her research widely in peer-reviewed journals, conferences, webinars, seminars and invited blog posts. Email: Omolabake.Fakunle@ed.ac.uk

Anne Pirrie, PhD, is a Reader in Education at the University of the West of Scotland. Her recent work has been in the area of critical universities studies, culminating in the publication of a monograph entitled *Virtue and the Quiet Art of Scholarship: Reclaiming the University* (Routledge, 2019). She has also published on fostering reflective practice in HE; and critiques of the student satisfaction agenda that has gained traction in the UK higher education arena in recent years. This has entailed exploring the interrelationship between two discrete discursive fields. Email: Anne.Pirrie@uws.ac.uk

Peer-Reviewed Article
Special Edition | Reflection and Reflective Thinking

© *Journal of International Students*
Volume 10, Issue S2 (2020), pp. 101-118
ISSN: 2162-3104 (Print), 2166-3750 (Online)
ojed.org/jis

Using Arts-Based Methods and Reflection to Support Postgraduate International Students' Wellbeing and Employability through Challenging Times

Marthy Watson
Georgina Barton
University of Southern Queensland, Australia

ABSTRACT

International students face many challenges when studying and living outside their home countries. These challenges are magnified when unexpected events occur such as COVID-19. Due to border closures, travel restrictions, quarantining and even job losses international students have particularly faced hardship in the first six months of the 2020 academic year in Australia. This paper reports on an arts-based research study that aimed to support international students to reflect on their studies and personal working lives during the COVID-19 global pandemic. The authors implemented a reflective process involving mindfulness and body mapping to support international students in expressing their experiences and feelings during this time. Results show that the international students gained a deeper understanding of what they experienced personally and how these experiences were both different and similar to their peers. The process enabled students to acknowledge and accept challenges faced as well as provided a safe avenue to do so. They reported the powerful nature of the arts-based methods in helping them think positively about their studies and future working lives.

Keywords: international students, reflection, wellbeing, challenges, future, employment

---

The outbreak of COVID-19 has impacted higher education students in varying ways worldwide. International students have particularly faced extraordinary challenges due to the global pandemic (Zhai & Du, 2020). In Australia, lockdowns of universities and workplaces nationwide as well as travel bans and closed borders to foreign travellers, including international students, has and will continue to challenge them into the foreseeable future. Such challenges have significantly disrupted international students' studies and increased their overall stress levels (Fischer, 2020).

Research shows that international students encounter a myriad of stressors when undertaking studies in a foreign country (Baik, Larcombe, & Brooker, 2019; Li, 2017; Li & Gasser, 2005; Tran & Gomes, 2017; Ward, 2009). The Orygen report (2017) for example, found that international students' levels of distress have increased over the past two decades (Orygen, 2017) due to a number of reasons including financial and lack of culturally-appropriate support which often leads to a limited sense of belonging (Glass, Kociolek, Wongtrirat, Lynch, & Cong, 2015). Similarly, Forbes-Mewett and Sawyer (2011) reported that international students are at an increased risk of mental health problems because of language difference and pressure to adjust to unfamiliar environments. Although students have access to university support such as face-to-face and online counselling when experiencing mental health issues, many students delay in seeking help because they feel embarrassed, afraid and anxious (Wynaden, Wichmann, & Murray, 2013).

Another barrier faced by international students is the lack of knowledge to access services (Eisenberg, Hunt, & Speer, 2012). Therefore, the need to adapt to unfamiliar environments and conditions, means that these students are at increased risk of developing mental health issues (Forbes-Mewett & Sawyer, 2011; Storrie, Ahern, & Tuckett, 2010) which can be compounded during times of uncertainty (Zhai & Du, 2020). Given the seriousness of issues such as these, international students may not achieve the results they are capable of or may even withdraw from their studies; which ultimately can impact on their success in seeking employment post-study.

As such, this paper reports on a project that sought to support international students in reflecting on the first semester of study during COVID-19. We implemented a range of arts-based workshops, both online and face-to-face that aimed to provide international students time to reflect on the challenges they were facing as well as share these experiences with others. The workshops aimed to improve international students' resilience and wellbeing through targeted activities designed around personal and professional reflection. It was hoped that these opportunities would support the international students to feel positive about their studies, ensuring success and hence future goals in employment. Therefore, the aims of the project were:

1. To provide an opportunity for international students to reflect on personal and/or professional challenges they faced during COVID-19; and
2. To support international students in finding effective ways to address challenges through their participation in reflective arts-based workshops.

ARTS-BASED REFLECTION

Life events can be described as those that significantly disturb daily routine (Luhmann, Hoffman, Eid, & Lucus, 2012). As highlighted, international students face certain challenges that their domestic peers do not. Issues such as language differences and difficulties, financial stress, and social isolation due to not being near friends and family (Barton, Hartwig, & Cain, 2015). Moving to another country and starting at a new university can be considered significant life events for international students. For this study, we focus on exploring the experiences of international students during the COVID-19 pandemic.

Reflection and reflective practice are well-recognized as assisting individuals and groups in coming to terms with certain life events, whereby one can consider what has happened, why it has happened the way it did, and how it might be different if experienced again (Bonanno, 2004). Many scholars note that reflection involves a number of phases and these have been extensively implemented in the higher education contexts (Gibbs, 1998; Johns, 2017; Kolb & Kolb, 2017). Benefits of explicitly teaching reflection to higher education students is critical for deep reflective practice to occur (Fergusson, Van Der Laan, & Baker, 2019; Barton & Ryan, 2013). Such practice can occur on either professional or personal levels. Fergusson, Allred and Dux (2018) share a micro-reflective cycle when contemplating personal challenges. They state that it operates on a personal level:

> …within the domain of the 'self' of an individual learner, on the level of thinking and doing. Thus, micro-reflective practice occurs within an individual's personal sphere of influence, centred on one's assumptions and beliefs, and is therefore intimate to personal learning (p. 291).

For the purpose of this paper we use Rodgers' (2002) framework, as did other authors in this special issue, to identify the process needed for international students to reflect on their first semester of study in an Australian university in 2020 (see below for further details). We found it necessary to implement a deeply robust framework in which to plan an arts-based reflective workshop for international students. Having such a conceptual framework as the basis of this work was imperative so that students were supported through an appropriate process in order to reflect deeply on this life event (Barton & Ryan, 2017) that will ultimately impact on their future employment prospects.

There is a growing body of evidence that points towards the importance of the role of arts-based practice in reflection and the improvement of health and wellbeing (Barton, McKay, Garvis & Sappa, 2019; Dodge, Daly, Huyton, & Sanders, 2012). Arts-based research is described as "a method designed to enlarge human understanding…and enable an individual to secure an empathic participation in the lives of other and in the situations studied" (Barone & Eisner, 2011, p. 8.) The approach has emerged over the last few decades using arts approaches such as dance, drama, song, poetry and visuals arts to assist people in understanding, examining and reflecting on their experiences. It is also noted that arts-based research uses stories, images, sounds, scenes and other sensory approaches to present research data (Ary et al., 2018). Such methods are "essential to the research process itself and central in formulating the research question, generating data, analysing data and presenting the research results" (Austin & Forinash, 2005, pp. 460–461).

Some research using arts-based methods stem from a cognitive or therapeutic base (Hertrampf & Wärja, 2017; Khan & Moss, 2017) however, it was not the intention of this study to use, for example, cognitive behavioural theory or medical intervention. This project used creative art-based practise to reflect on and process international students' experiences during the COVID crisis.

To date, there has not been a significant research focus on the impact of stress on the wellbeing and resilience of international students in major life events (Richardson, 2002). Studies in Scandinavia, Australia and the USA have found arts-based practices enhance the individual's capacity to resolve social issues and to assist in recovery from natural disasters (Clift, 2012; Cox et al., 2010; Ewing, 2010). For example, the Big hART project in Australia used arts-based activities to work with tenants in the NSW Department of Housing to help participants to tell stories through photographic portraits, music and performance theatre. The study found that these activities created an opportunity for participant's lives to be validated and to encourage conditions that decreased violence and isolation (Wright & Palmer, 2007, p. 6). Similarly, O'Connor (2020) led an arts-based project in Australia called the *Banksia Initiative* to support teachers and schools during the bushfire disaster in early 2020. The project provided participatory arts-based methods to restore individual, community and national wellbeing during and after a disaster and strengthen social support to help people to "build critical hope" (Arts Health Network, 2020). A National Arts and Health Framework developed by the Australian Health and Cultural Ministers, acknowledges the wellbeing benefits through participation in creative engagement with the arts (Health Ministers & Cultural Ministers, 2014). These engagements, for example, can be used as a means for community recovery and regeneration after trauma and to solve health and wellbeing problems by inspiring new ways of thinking (Harms, Brady, Wood, & Silard, 2018).

It is timely to understand and gather evidence on the wellbeing and resilience of international students in this critical life event. Acknowledging and identifying the impact of this life event will allow universities to be prepared to improve international students' wellbeing and support them in personal, social, and cultural growth to successfully complete their studies.

RESEARCH DESIGN USING RODGERS' REFLECTIVE FRAMEWORK

To be present in, and see, the world means to pay attention to the detailed minute happenings around us. As researchers employing arts-based activities to teach reflection, we argue it is necessary for students to "slow down" to observe these minute happenings to ensure critical and transformative reflection occurs (Rodgers, 2002). As such we developed a creatively reflective workshop, as a way of conducting research (Ørngreen & Levinsen, 2017), that aimed to support international students in slowing down to reflect on their lived experience to facilitate change and improve wellbeing. The workshop provided a vehicle to provoke the international students to use their senses to reflect on their learning and challenging times such as during the COVID pandemic.

In our workshop, the international students participated in a number of arts-based reflective processes including photo elicitation (McKay & Barton, 2018), meditative reflection by focusing on the senses (Siegel, 2018), and a body mapping exercise (MacCormack & Draper, 1987). By utilising these methods, deep reflection was possible through prompting and eliciting rich information (Boydell et al., 2012). We now highlight how these arts-based processes align with Rodgers' (2002) four principles underlying the reflective cycle.

The first principle deals with the idea that the primary text for reflection must be centred on the individual's own experience (Kolb, 1984). We acknowledge how international students bring with them to their studies their own unique stories due to differing cultural beliefs, language and the ways of being (Ryan & Hellmundt, 2007). We therefore began the workshop with each student drawing a card from a selection of motivational quotes and images. Students were then invited to introduce themselves one at a time and use the quote and image on the card to focus their introduction through a technique called photo elicitation. Photo elicitation is a visual sociological methodology used in qualitative research (McKay & Barton, 2018). It uses images to evoke responses from participants. By listening to each participant, we were drawn into their world of experience and with respect, the uniqueness of each individual was shared.

In Rodgers' second phase, the process to move away from ordinary thought (Dewey, 1933) and reactivity to challenging issues was implemented through a mediation exercise. To introduce "slowness", we led the students through a mindful meditation session where they visualised the wheel of awareness (Siegel, 2018). This wheel has a central hub, an outer rim, and four quadrants in between. This metaphor embodies how the mind is structured. The hub represents experiences of awareness such as the feeling of calmness, perspective openness and peacefulness. The four quadrants represent: the *sensory awareness* of what we can see, hear, smell, taste and touch; *bodily awareness* and what we can physically sense; *mental activities* such as feelings, thoughts and memories; and the *interconnectedness* with things outside ourselves such as other people and other things.

By connecting with these experiences during the meditation, the activity fostered a sense of connection and awareness with the individual and their connection with the world (Altinyelken, Hoek, & Jiang, 2019). After the meditation, students were encouraged to write down the thoughts and feelings experienced during the mediation session on a hard copy of the wheel. This served as a starting point to focus their reflection on specific events and connections in their lives (Hendrickson, Rosen, & Aune, 2011). These words, symbols or images were then transferred to a map of the body that communicated the richness of their life story as a visual representation.

The third principle is guided by the notion of community of respect among participants (Rodgers, 2002). Body mapping is a means of visual storytelling, where individuals visually share their reflections (Botha, 2017). Unlike an interview where only the interviewer is present, the body mapping process is revealed and shared with others. There was a sharing of reflective practice as students put marks, images and words on their body map. Students continuously throughout the workshop, revealed and shared their stories with other students and workshop facilitators. In our workshops, we found that the mundane conversation between participants revealed the depth of reflection as students talked about events in their lives. Herein lies the recognition that their stories were not insignificant and were worthy of sharing. At the completion of the workshop, each student reflected on their body map in front of the other students. Body mapping becomes a story of "This is who I am, this is my story, and this is what is important to me." An integral part of the workshop was to value and foster mutual respect for each other's stories.

Rodgers (2002) applied a critical understanding of the value of feedback as the fourth principle underlying the reflective cycle. Feedback is associated with improving student learning, where the teacher is merely telling students what is right and wrong and how might improve. This narrow view of feedback relegates feedback to a one-way transmission process (Nicol, 2010; Sadler, 2010). Hence our view that the workshop's purpose was not used to provide "feedback" by facilitators to students on their reflections and artwork. Rodgers (2002) proposed structured feedback as a way for a teacher to see through the eyes of their students and become a partner in the inquiry. She continued to say that teachers as reflective practitioners start to realise the way, for example, learning materials, activities and even classroom setup can offer opportunities to observe student learning.

The arts-based workshops were offered both online (1 hour x 1) and face-to-face (3 hours x 2) on two different campuses within the university. We planned the online workshop to be shorter given our knowledge of online fatigue experienced by participants in past projects. Each workshop was held 4 weeks apart, therefore over three months throughout Semester 2, 2020. Participants were international students who were currently enrolled in higher degree research programs such as master's or doctoral level studies. An invitation was emailed to all students across the university through a regular events notification. The online workshop was attended by 12 international students and the face-to-face workshops were attended by 8 and 7 participants (it is important to note that strict COVID-19 hygiene practices were carried out during the face-to-face workshops including a limit on how many students could attend).

The arts-based and reflective workshops were developed based on our experience conducting research in the arts and on reflection (Barton et al., 2019) as well as our work with international students (Barton et al., 2017). Our position as researchers also involved our role as supervisors and academics. Most of the students who attended the workshops were from other faculties across the university but one of the authors had two of her doctoral students attend. We positioned ourselves as participant-observers in the face-to-face workshops as we created artwork alongside the students. All ethical protocols were carried out appropriately including formal approvals to conduct this study.

Our workshops were structured so that the international students felt comfortable and safe to share their experiences with each other. We also conducted semi-structured interviews after the workshops with students who provided consent to do so. For example, asking questions such as the ones below, so we were able to experience the way in which students were present in the world.

- What symbols/images have you chosen to describe your emotions and journey as an international student at USQ and Australia?
- Can you explain the meaning of your symbol and slogan?
- Where on your body map would you like to place these symbols and why?

These questions opened up the discussion between facilitators and students, and students and students, but there were also moments of silence for the participants to ponder quietly, the meanings of each other's work.

Lastly, Rodgers (2002) claims that "student learning should guide teaching and practice. Reflection as a practice should focus on the response to student learning and not be seen as a checklist of teaching behaviours" (p. 7). Our workshop endeavoured to break the chain of checking in for learning by teachers and engaged in activities that used reflection as a response to student learning. As reflection and learning are intertwined and described as "the process whereby knowledge is created through the transformation of experience" (Kolb, 1984, p. 38), we understood that this approach provided a way of questioning and sharing underlying beliefs (Moon, 2013; Schön, 1983). Through reflective practice, we invited the whole human being into the learning situation.

The analytic methods used to comprehend our data were thematic and visual analysis. We used inductive thematic analysis to understand the international student interviews and oral reflections made throughout the workshop. We also used a semiotic framework to analyse the final works of art created by the international students. According to Hodgetts, Chamberlain, and Groot (2012) visual methods "provide a basis for understanding hardship…in relation to situational, societal, material and relational contexts" (p. 299). Such methods can be used to reveal information from research participants and/or be the result of data collection including drawings and other artworks (Gleeson, 2012). Our analysis involves the selection of specific aspects in the art that the international students chose to discuss more deeply in their interviews and reflections. Consequently, we first describe the work then share these features in the hope that the international students' voices are strongly present.

FINDINGS AND DISCUSSION

In analysing the semi-structured interviews and visual body maps, an over-arching theme speaking to the difficulties associated with being an international post-graduate student were identified. Within this theme, three sub-themes emerged during analysis. They were isolation during COVID-19; a need for a sense of belonging to the community, and the importance of self-reflection through arts-based approaches to understand challenges faced. As students strongly identified with their body maps created in the workshop, they felt at ease to speak to their artwork during the interviews. In mapping the visual analysis of the body maps, these themes were visible on the body maps in the form of semiotics such as symbols and icons, colours, cultural representations and written language.

Isolation during COVID-19

In Australia, international students faced the suspension of face-to-face classes and the move to online teaching in March 2020 to curb the spread of the COVID-19 virus. Participants described the lockdown as "very unfortunate" (Participant 2) and spoke about the stress and anxiety the event had on the personal lives and studies. Most students felt that the lockdown at first did not affect their study. One student commented: "To be honest, I do not think it affected my study at all because it allowed me to study more because I was in my apartment all the time" (Participant 4). As time progressed and the lockdown measures intensified, the students felt the isolation more acutely. On an academic level students felt isolated and lonely. Two students commented on the isolation and the effect it had on them:

> There were days when I will be able to work, there are days when I'm just so demotivated. And it was... I think I spent a whole month to adjust to working from home because I had to go buy a table. The university allowed us to take computers home and eventually I got into a routine. *Participant #3*

and

> Working from home is as a PhD student is very difficult. Sometimes I feel bored, sometimes sleepy, but I am not coming to office frequently. Working from in home has greatly affected my study and is not good for my progress. My PhD will be completed in early 2022, but due to COVID, maybe it will now be shifted six months later. *Participant #2*

The lockdown due to COVID-19 also had adverse consequences on students' personal and professional lives and in particular students who worked to support their studies in Australia. One student demonstrated this effect as she explained:

The first thing is that I lost my job because of the COVID-19. I used to work in the shopping centre, in a tea shop and [large store]. After the COVID-19 they say they don't need too many people work here. So they just fired me because I just worked there part time. They just fired me, and I don't have any income because I am supporting myself. It's a little bit hard for me. I try to find another job, but it's very hard for me to find a part time job during this time. *Participant #5*

These reflections on the effects of COVID-19 on their lives as international students were reimagined on their body maps. *Figure 1* shows a body map of a person with a white torso and blue and black covering on the legs. Of importance here is the bottom part of the pair of legs. The student reflected on his current situation and explained that he placed the black striped material on the bottom half of the legs and made holes in them to show, although his legs are strong, the isolation and uncertainty of COVID-19 is weakening him. The participant in this image also likened the striped material to his thesis drafts and the holes represented the edits his supervisors did to his work.

Figure 1: "Weak legs"

On a personal level, the students felt the isolation more intensely. Many students have planned trips to their home country to visit family and friends. These trips are now on hold until international borders reopen. Many of the students are married and their partner and children are in their home country. Two students remarked:

When the lockdown was announced, so prior to the lockdown, I bought my tickets and everything to go to Fiji in April for my sister's wedding. But then when the lockdown was announced, then I had to cancel everything. *Participant #1*

and

I'm so scared of what's going to happen to my marriage right now, because we tend to spend a lot of time apart and now, I can't go home. So sometimes it is like, okay, my husband is trying, we are good. And then sometimes I feel like we are disconnected. *Participant #3*

The higher degree students also were worried about what would happen in terms of employment once they completed their studies. As post-graduate students they were all very passionate about their areas of study and making a difference in their communities. Their love of their home countries was a large focus in their reflective artworks.

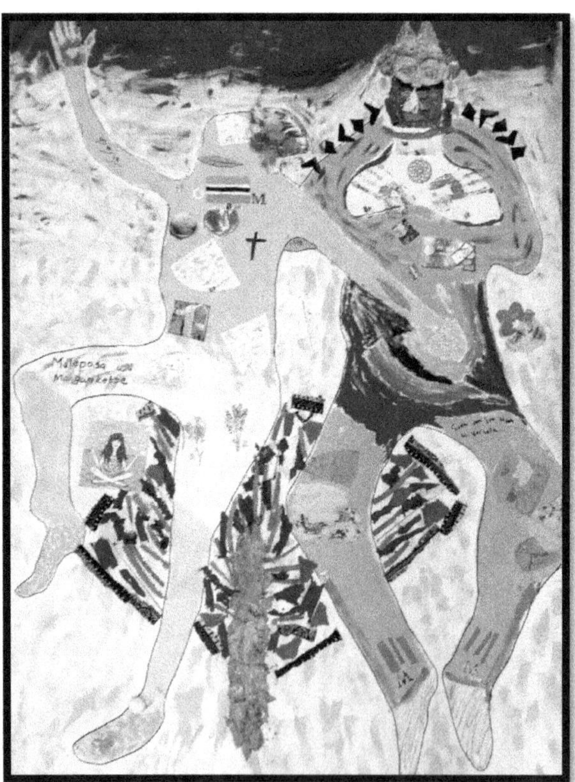

Figure 2: "My red heart"

These fears are manifested on the student's body map as she drew a red heart on her chest, denoting the love she has for her husband (Figure 2 on the left-hand side of the canvas). Although the red signifies love, the red could also be the signifier for the loss of not being near her husband and the fear of how the COVID-19 pandemic will affect her marriage.

A sense of belonging in the community

The sense of belonging to a community and establishing friendships were perceived as essential factors by all participants. A study by Ramsey et al. (2007) showed that international students struggled to find opportunities to integrate into the local community and form emotional and social companionship. One student commented:

In Fiji, I have got lots of friends, so mostly at least once a week I meet them. But here I have two friends. It was hard to make friends because I didn't have any classes and I did not know anyone in Queensland or the places near, because once the lockdown started, they (Australians) all went to their homes from the apartments where I live. *Participant #1*

It was especially difficult for students to form friendships, pursue existing friendships and to become part of society after the lockdown of the USQ campus in late March 2020. Although participants acknowledged that they hoped for social inclusion and wanted to make local friends, the reality was very different. After the lockdown, it was even more challenging to make friends as the interaction that took place between students in class disappeared as classes moved online. The COVID-19 lockdown prompted Australian students, who lived in university residences, to move back to their families.

The participants displayed a real sense of longing to be part of the fabric of society and contribute to society. Students expressed the desire to join university groups and community volunteering activities as one of the students stated that "I want to input my energy to working with the community as this can be helpful for us because we can mix with them" (Participant 2). One student mentioned that he had already donated blood three times since arriving in Australia. This action of giving back to the community was very fulfilling for him and made him feel part of society.

The lack of opportunities to develop intercultural friendships can also play a role in developing and advancing students' English language capacity (Martin, 2020). The students also admitted that it was challenging to establish interpersonal relationships with Australian students as an international student. Most of their friends were either international students or students from their own home country. Participants saw interaction with English speaking students as an opportunity to improve their English and learn about Australian culture.

However, students all agreed that they had received support from their academic supervisors and that the university was "always there for us" (Participant 1). Students mentioned how supervisors and lecturers had regular contact with them, mostly weekly and how they appreciated this support. Many students lived in university residence and shared accommodation with other students. Because of the prolonged periods spent together during lockdown, it was revealed that their housemates were a great source of support for them. Participants also mentioned that they started doing exercises in their flats to combat anxiety and depression. One student commented:

> And even during lockdown, even though I was not able to go to gym, I was being able to do things, follow YouTube videos, just work out in the house. It wasn't very effective, especially in terms of getting benefits, but it was something. *Participant #5*

Participants also spoke about the support they received from their families in their home country. They mentioned that regular Skype and Messenger conversations kept their spirits up but also realised that it would be a while before they would see each other.

The importance of self-reflection

The students self-identified that they valued the chance to reflect on their studies and recognised the importance of reflection as an essential part of wellbeing. Barton et al. (2019) argue that arts-based activities contribute to resilience and wellbeing as it provides agency through foregrounding students' voices. Similarly, research has shown that expressing feelings through arts-based methods allows participants to access a less invasive and safe way to reflect on self and others (Dodge et al., 2012). In addition, arts-based activities encouraged communication that exposed ideas, emotions and feelings that previously might not have been expressed.

International students are at a high risk of psychological problems such as stress and anxiety (Rosenthal et al., 2008). However, Barton et al. (2019) argue that the "arts can trigger different ways of knowing and thinking about situations that require reflection for advancement (p. 1). Students felt that the reflective body mapping activity assisted them "to break depression" (Participant 2). The workshop allowed them to reflect on their journey through the lockdown of COVID-19 as international students in Australia.

In the interviews, we asked students about the importance of reflection, especially using arts-based activities such as body mapping. The students pointed out that the body mapping activity not only helped them to meet and connect with other people but also to understand and reflect on their journey. The non-judgemental space provided by the workshop to express their feeling and emotions was considered significant by the participants. They felt that they could express themselves without being judged. The activity assisted them to reflect on their personal and educational journey and at the same time to improve communication, connect with others and learn from and about other people. Presented below are the reflections from three participants:

> Reflection 1:
> It [the reflection] allowed us to engage with others and learn from others. For example, if you see this body art, we can learn about different people just by looking at art. It also allows us to put things which we cannot write or cannot describe in the form of paintings. Even though no one else will understand what you have put, as long as you understand you have put your message out. And it is a kind of challenge if anyone, without me explaining, if anyone can point

those things out, then it would be quite interesting to see if people can think the same way as you. Doing this also allows us to disengage from the daily studies, which are quite stressful now in these times. *Participant #2*

Reflection 2:
I know more people here in USQ and I made more friends and I was so amazed by [another participant's] work because I can feel the totally different thinking mode between us. I can feel the difference between us. I can feel like a kind of foreign culture from his work. But for me, it's very hard for me to imagine his work, but when he presents his work, I feel it is very different from other's work. I think I know more about difference, the meaning of difference, especially on a thinking mode. And just now, before I came here, we had really long conversation about Australian life, culture and language. I think I learned more about this country and the culture here and as well as the language. *Participant #5*

Reflection 3:
It helped me to connect with people, make new friends. It was interesting to work with another person, get their ideas, to ask them "What do you think?". Having somebody there who we can share ideas with. It made us express our feelings freely, especially with the painting without being judged. Most of the time our lives we follow this protocol, especially with writing, follow this, do these things this way. But with the creative workshop, we can just be yourself. You can think about your situation. *Participant #3*

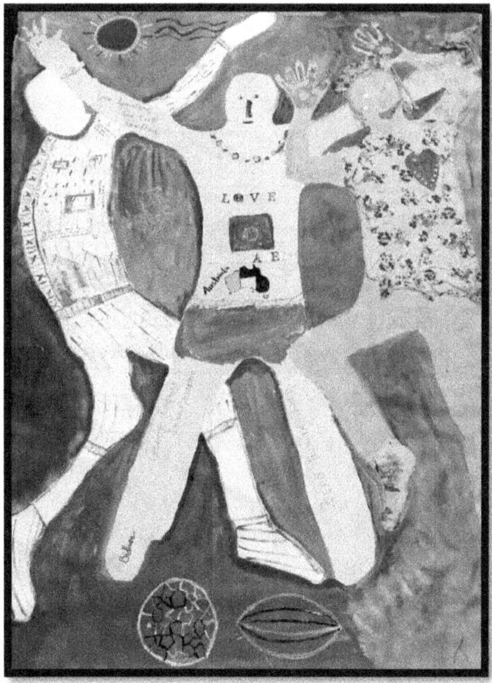

Figure 3: "Move it"

112

The body maps in Figure 3 depicted an appearance of movement, activity and animation. Although the participants revealed that depression and anxiety were part of their journey as international students, they felt that through expressing their feelings and emotions through reflection, they could manage stress and anxiety. One student described his need for reflection accordingly:

> I think it is really important to have such reflective experiences as international students, because it enables us to connect with other people and it also allows us to disengage from the daily studies, which can be quite stressful at times, and to show something of ourselves as people. *Participant #1*

IMPLICATIONS AND CONCLUSION

It was clear that the reflective arts-based workshops provided a much-needed opportunity for international students undertaking post-graduate studies to reflect on their experiences during an international crisis—COVID-19. The varied and multimodal approaches to reflection provided the necessary tools for the international students to reflect in a way that was culturally responsive and appropriate (Barton & Ryan, 2020). Rodgers' framework provided a robust way to develop an approach for the reflective arts-based workshops as well as a way to make sense of the artworks and interview data. Acknowledging and valuing the international students' own personal and professional experiences prior to and during their study was important for the students to feel comfortable with each other or as Rodgers' puts it a 'community of respect'. Using images and motivational quotes initially enabled the students to share their own stories and motivations to be a post-graduate student. It allowed them to reflect on the challenges faced during COVID-19 and how this might eventually impact on their capacity to find their employment of choice post-study.

Further, the mindfulness activity, through the guided meditation, ensured the international students had a way of 'moving away from ordinary thought' as well as providing a prompt by which to develop their artworks. Without such creative approaches it would have been difficult for the international students to reflect deeply and reveal their inner feelings and thoughts related to their professional and personal lives (Moffatt et al., 2016). In addition, the artworks were appropriate vehicles by which the international students could express specific instances in their lives, their cultural and linguistic diversity, and things that mattered to them most; which were heightened during the global pandemic.

Implications

It is apparent that ongoing and continued support for international postgraduate students is critical during critical happenings and challenges. We acknowledge that international students studying higher degrees by research would receive support from their supervisors, however, we argue that other systems of support are needed from a range of staff located across the university community so that all needs are met. Such support should value the fact that international students need to feel a sense of belonging and community as per Rodgers' third principle whereby respect is at the core. Our study showed that our participants had, to date, limited access to others that were experiencing similar situations. They greatly valued the opportunity to meet other international students who were studying master's degrees or doctorates.

In addition, reflective work with international students must value cultural or linguistic differences and provide the platform for both students and facilitators to reflect and learn from each other. As such, we found that a more informal approach to sharing encouraged growth through the reflective process itself. It allowed participants to first, name and recognise challenges and then second, appreciate and embed appropriate strategies for change and improved wellbeing to occur. We noticed that international students then felt more positive about their future and prospective employment post-study.

REFERENCES

Altinyelken, H. K., Hoek, L., & Jiang, L. (2019). Improving the psychosocial wellbeing of international students: The relevance of mindfulness. *British Journal of Guidance & Counselling*, 1-13.

Arts Health Network (2020). *About the banksia initiative: recovering, rebuilding, reimagining*. Retrieved from: https://www.artshealthnetwork.com.au/about-the-banksia-initiative-recovering-rebuilding-reimagining/

Ary, D., Jacobs, L. C., Irvine, C. K. S., & Walker, D. (2018). *Introduction to research in education*. Cengage Learning.

Austin, D., & Forinash, M. (2005). Arts-based research. *Music Therapy Research*, *2*, 458-471.

Baik, C., Larcombe, W., & Brooker, A. (2019). How universities can enhance student mental wellbeing: the student perspective. *Higher Education Research & Development*, *38*(4), 674-687. DOI: 10.1080/07294360.2019.1576596

Barone, T., & Eisner, E. W. (2011). *Arts based research*. Sage.

Barton G. M., Hartwig, K., & Cain, M. (2015). International students' experience of practicum in teacher education: An exploration through internationalisation and professional socialisation. *Australian Journal of Teacher Education*, *40*(8), 149-163.

Barton, G. M., Hartwig, K., Bennett, D., Cain, M., Campbell, M., Ferns, S., Jones, L., Joseph, D., Kavanagh, M., Kelly, A., Larkin, I., O'Connor, E., Podorova, A., Tangen, D., & Westerveld, M. (2017). Work placement for international students: A model of effective practice. In G. M. Barton & K. Hartwig (Eds.), *professional learning in the workplace for international students: Exploring theory and practice*, (pp. 13-34). Springer.

Barton, G. M., McKay, L., Garvis, S., & Sappa, V (2019). Introduction: Defining and theorising key concepts of resilience and well-being and arts-based research. In L. McKay, G. M. Barton, S. Garvis & V. Sappa (Eds.), *Arts-based research, resilience and well-being across the lifespan*, (pp. 1-12). Palgrave.

Barton, G. M., & Ryan, M. (2013). Multimodal approaches to reflective teaching and assessment in higher education: a cross disciplinary approach in Creative Industries. *Higher Education Research and Development*, *33*(3), 409-424.

Barton, G. M., & Ryan, M.E. (2017). Reflection and reflective practice for international students and their supervisors in context. In G. M. Barton & K.

Hartwig (Eds.), *Professional learning in the workplace for international students: Exploring theory and practice,* (pp. 93-110). Springer.

Barton, G. M., & Ryan, M. (2020). What does reflection look and feel like for international students? An exploration of reflective thinking, reflexivity and employability. *Journal of International Students, 10*(S2), 1-15.

Bonanno, G. A. (2004). Loss, trauma, and human resilience: Have we underestimated the human capacity to thrive after extremely aversive events? *American Psychologist*, 59, 20-28.

Botha, C. S. (2017). Using metaphoric body-mapping to encourage reflection on the developing identity of pre-service teachers. *South African Journal of Education, 37*(3).

Boydell, K. M., Volpe, T., Cox, S., Katz, A., Dow, R., Brunger, F., & Wong, L. (2012). Ethical challenges in arts-based health research. *The International Journal of the Creative Arts in Interdisciplinary Practice, 11*(1), 1-17.

Clift, S. (2012). Creative arts as a public health resource: moving from practice-based research to evidence-based practice. *Perspectives in Public Health* 132, 3, 120 – 127

Cox, S. M., Lafrenière, D., Brett-MacLean, P., Collie, K., Cooley, N., Dunbrack, J. & Frager, G. (2010). Tipping the iceberg? The state of arts and health in Canada, Arts & Health: *An International Journal for Research, Policy and Practice*, 2:2, 109-124.

Dodge, R., Daly, A., Huyton, J., & Sanders, L. (2012). The challenge of defining well-being. *International Journal of Wellbeing, 2*(3), 222-235. doi:10.5502/ijw.v2i3.4

Eisenberg, D., Hunt, J. & Speer, N. (2012). Help seeking for mental health on college campuses: review of evidence and next steps for research and practice. *Harv Rev Psychiatry*, 20, 222-232.

Ewing, R. (2010). *The arts and Australian education: Realising potential*. ACER.

Fergusson, L., Allred, T., & Dux, T. (2018). Work-based learning and research for mid-career professionals: Professional studies in Australia. *Interdisciplinary Journal of E-skills and Lifelong Learning*, 14, 1–17.

Fergusson, L., Van Der Laan, L., & Baker, S. (2019). Reflective practice and work-based research: a description of micro-and macro-reflective cycles. *Reflective Practice, 20*(2), 289-303.

Fischer, K. (2020). Confronting the seismic impact of COVID-19: The need for research. *Journal of International Students, 10*(2), 211.

Forbes-Mewett, H. & Sawyer, A. M. (2011). Mental health issues amongst international students in Australia: perspectives from professionals at the coal-face. The Australian Sociological Association Conference Local Lives/ Global Networks. University of Newcastle New South Wales.

Gibbs, G. (1988). *Learning by doing: A guide to teaching learning methods*. Oxford Brookes University.

Glass, C. R., Kociolek, E., Wongtrirat, R., Lynch, R. J., & Cong, S. (2015). Uneven experiences: The impact of student-faculty interactions on international students' sense of belonging. *Journal of International Students, 5*(4), 353-367.

Gleeson, K. (2012). Polytextual thematic analysis for visual data. In P. Reavey (Ed.), *Visual methods in Psychology: Using and Interpreting Images in Qualitative Research*, (pp. 314-323). Psychology Press.

Harms, P. D., Brady, L., Wood, D., & Silard, A. (2018). Resilience and well-being. In E. Diener, S. Oishi, & L. Tay (Eds.), *Handbook of well-Being*. DEF Publishers.

Health Ministers and Cultural Ministers (2014). *National arts and health framework*, Perth, 2014, http://mcm.arts.gov.au/article/national-arts-and-health-framework-released

Hendrickson, B., Rosen, D., & Aune, R. K. (2011). An analysis of friendship networks, social connectedness, homesickness, and satisfaction levels of international students. *International journal of intercultural relations, 35*(3), 281-295.

Hertrampf, R. S., & Wärja, M. (2017). The effect of creative arts therapy and arts medicine on psychological outcomes in women with breast or gynecological cancer: A systematic review of arts-based interventions. *The Arts in Psychotherapy, 56*, 93-110.

Hodgetts, D., Chamberlain, K., & Groot, S. (2012). Reflections on the visual in community research and action. In P. Reavey (Ed.), *Visual methods in psychology: Using and interpreting images in qualitative research*, (pp. 299-313). Psychology Press.

Johns, C. (Ed.). (2017). *Becoming a reflective practitioner, 5th ed.* Wiley.

Khan, W. U., & Moss, H. (2017). Increasing public health awareness of and capacity for arts-based therapy in medicine. *Jama Neurology, 74*(9), 1029-1030.

Kolb, D. A. (1984). Experiential learning: Experience as the source of learning and development. Prentice–Hall.

Kolb, A. Y. & Kolb, D. A. (2017). *The experiential educator: Principles and practices of experiential learning*. EBLS Press.

Li, H. (2017). Academic integration of mainland Chinese students in Germany. *Social Inclusion, 5*(1), 80–92. doi: 10.17645/si.v5i1.824

Li, A., & Gasser, M. B. (2005). Predicting Asian international students' sociocultural adjustment: A test of two mediation models. *International Journal of Intercultural Relations, 29*, 561–576.10.1016/j.ijintrel.2005.06.003

Luhmann, M., Hofmann, W., Eid, M., & Lucas, R. E. (2012). Subjective well-being and adaptation to life events: a meta-analysis. *Journal of personality and social psychology, 102*(3), 592.

MacCormack, C. P., & Draper, A. (1987). Social and cognitive aspects of female sexuality in Jamaica. In C. MacCormack & A. Draper (Eds.), *Social and Cognitive Aspects of Female Sexuality in Jamaica,* (pp. 143-65).Routledge.

McKay, L., & Barton, G. M. (2018). Exploring how arts-based reflection can support teachers' resilience and wellbeing. *Teaching and Teacher Education, 75*, 356-365. https://doi.org/10.1016/j.tate.2018.07.012

Martin, F. (2020). *Chinese international students' wellbeing in Australia: The road to recovery*. The University of Melbourne.

Moffatt, A., Barton, G., & Ryan, M. (2016). Multimodal reflection for creative facilitators: An approach to improving self-care. *Reflective Practice, 17*(6), 762-778.

Moon, J. A. (2013). *Reflection in learning and professional development: Theory and practice.*Routledge.

Nicol, D. (2010). From monologue to dialogue: improving written feedback processes in mass higher education. *Assessment & Evaluation in Higher Education, 35*(5), 501-517.

O'Connor, P. (2020). *An arts-based approach to student resilience.* Retrieved from: https://www.teachermagazine.com.au/articles/an-arts-based-approach-to-student-resilience

Ørngreen R and Levinsen K. (2017). Workshops as a research methodology. *The Electronic Journal of e-Learning, 15*(1), 70-81.

Richardson, G .E. (2002). The metatheory of resilience and resiliency, *Journal of Clinical Psychology*, 58 (3), 307-321.

Rodgers, C. (2002). Defining reflection: Another look at John Dewey and reflective thinking. *Teachers college record, 104*(4), 842-866.

Rosenthal, D., Russell, J., & Thomson, G. (2008). The health and well-being of international Students at an Australian university. *Higher Education, 55,* 51-67.

Ryan, J., & Hellmundt, S. (2007). Maximising international students' 'cultural capital'. In J. Carroll & J. Ryan (Eds.), *Teaching International Students: Improving Learning for all,* (pp. 25-28). Routledge.

Sadler, D. R. (2010). Beyond feedback: Developing student capability in complex appraisal. *Assessment & Evaluation in Higher Education, 35*(5), 535-550.

Schön, D. A. (1983). *The reflective practitioner: How professionals think in action.* Basic Books, Inc.

Siegel, D. (2018). *Aware: The science and practice of presence--the groundbreaking meditation practice.* Penguin.

Storrie, K., Ahern, K. & Tuckett, A. (2010). A systematic review: Students with mental health problems—A growing problem. *International Journal of Nursing Practice*, 16, 1-6.

The Orygen report (2017). *Innovation driving reform: Annual report, 2017.* Parkville, Victoria, Australia: The National Centre of Excellence in youth Mental Health.

Tran, L. T., & Gomes, C. (2017). Student mobility, connectedness and identity. In *International student connectedness and identity* (pp. 1-11). Springer.

Ward, C., Masgoret, A.-M. and Gezentsvey, M. (2009). Investigating attitudes toward international students: Program and policy implications for social integration and international education. *Social Issues and Policy Review*, 3: 79-102. doi:10.1111/j.1751-2409.2009.01011.x

Wright, P.P., & Palmer, D. (2007). *People now me for something positive: An evaluation of Big hART's work at the John Northcote Estate*: Murdock University.

Wynaden, D., Wichmann, H., & Murray, S. (2013). A synopsis of the mental health concerns of university students: Results of a text-based online survey from one Australian university. *Higher Education Research & Development, 32*(5), 846-860.

Zhai, Y., & Du, X. (2020). Mental health care for international Chinese students affected by the COVID-19 outbreak. *The Lancet Psychiatry*, *7*(4), e22.

BIOGRAPHIES

MARTHY WATSON is a Lecturer at the University of Southern Queensland. She has been an arts educator for over 20 years and taught the arts in secondary and primary schools South Africa, New Zealand and Australia. Marthy has extensive experience in leading and developing course materials in the area of literacy and arts education. She has worked on numerous research projects supporting culturally and linguistically diverse communities. Her current research focuses on reflective practice thought arts-based learning. She strongly advocates for the arts and regularly presents at conferences and arts workshops in schools. Email: marthy.watson@usq.edu.au

GEORGINA BARTON, PhD, is a Professor of literacies and pedagogy in the School of Education at the University of Southern Queensland, Brisbane, Australia. Before being an academic, Georgina taught in schools for over 20 years including teaching English in South India with Australian Volunteers International. She has been an acting principal, coordinator of international students, and a lead teacher in the area of literacy. Georgina also has extensive experience in teaching the arts in schools and universities and often utilises the arts to support students' literacy learning outcomes. She has over 120 publications in the areas of the arts and literacy. She is an editor of a book titled *Professional Learning for International Students: Exploring Theory and Practice.* Email: georgina.barton@usq.edu.au

---

www.ingramcontent.com/pod-product-compliance
Lightning Source LLC
Chambersburg PA
CBHW051424150726

48000CB00005B/1946